The Minnesota DIVORCE REVOLUTION

A PLAIN ENGLISH EXPLANATION OF CURRENT MINNESOTA DIVORCE LAW

by:
Jeanette A. Frederickson
& Cort C. Holten

Regency Press, Inc. Minneapolis, Minnesota.

Library of Congress Catalog Number: 86-61174
ISBN: 0-9622587-0-9

The authors and publisher specifically disclaim any liability, loss or risk, personal or otherwise, which is incurred as a consequence, directly or indirectly, of the use and application of any of the contents of this work. Furthermore, questions relevant to the practice of law or accounting should be addressed to a member of those professions.

Acknowledgements

A special thanks must be extended to those who helped this project progress. Our appreciation goes to Cheryl Lennon, Susan Oliphant, Mary Sargent, Jodie Ryan, Joanna Haugen and Nancy Silesky. Their assistance and various skills were invaluable.

Foreword

The *Minnesota Divorce Revolution* is an excellent explanation of current Minnesota divorce law, including the many changes which have occurred in recent years. Using understandable language, this book enables the reader to examine the divorce process and helps anyone experiencing a divorce to become an active, knowledgeable participant.

It provides invaluable information regarding:

- property division
- spousal maintenance
- child custody and support
- violence in the family

and other important topics.

A.M. (Sandy) Keith
Minnesota Supreme Court Justice

It's difficult and frightening to end a marriage. Having to turn to the legal system with its special rules and language for marriage dissolution can make ending the marriage even more difficult and frightening.

The Minnesota Divorce Revolution reduces the mystique of divorce and can help you better understand the law, the language and the process. This book has been needed for a long time.

Mary D. Winter
Chief Judge of Family Court
in Hennepin County, Minnesota

About the Authors

JEANETTE A. FREDERICKSON is an attorney with Chestnut & Brooks, P.A., specializing in family law. She served two clerkships with the Minnesota Court of Appeals for The Honorable Edward Parker and The Honorable Doris Huspeni, holds an advanced degree in psychology, and taught in the field of special education for 15 years. Her first published book described the impact of the handicap of deafness on a family. *Life After Deaf* was published by the National Association of the Deaf in 1985. Ms. Frederickson has one college-aged daughter.

CORT C. HOLTEN is a partner in the law firm of Chestnut & Brooks, P.A., practicing in a variety of civil law areas. A former criminal defense lawyer, Mr. Holten joined the firm in 1981, and in 1987 he successfully represented the petitioner/wife in what became the famous Minnesota Supreme Court landmark decision, *Nardini v. Nardini.* He is the author of numerous articles for legal journals, a specialist in government affairs at the state legislature, and the father of two sons.

The law firm of Chestnut & Brooks, P.A. is located at 3700 Piper Jaffray Tower, 222 South Ninth Street, in Minneapolis, Minnesota, and has been serving clients for over a quarter of a century.

Contents

Introduction

This book is designed as a practical guide for the divorcing Minnesotan. Family law in Minnesota has undergone revolutionary changes in recent years. From 1984 forward, the volume and complexity of the changes have left many Minnesotans in the dark about current divorce law. The resulting confusion is complicated by the emotional stress of divorce which triggers fears of material loss, abandonment and guilt. By its very nature, divorce places both parties at the mercy of a system which has its own language and procedures and which can move people like pawns through a complex process. This book is designed to alleviate some of that confusion. It should put you in the habit of asking questions and enable you to become a more informed client. We hope this book can reduce your insecurity and frustration by involving you in the process and by de-mystifying some of the language.

In 1986, in Minnesota, there were 14,426 divorces and 34,199 marriages. Odds are that you, a family member, friend or co-worker will be touched by some issue resulting from a divorce: child custody, support, maintenance or property settlements.

Many of the recent changes in our laws reflect changing societal values. Before 1973 the law took a rather paternalistic view toward divorce requiring that an applicant for divorce prove that some marital misconduct entitled one party to end the marriage. Typical grounds for divorce included adultery, desertion and mental or physical cruelty.

In 1974, Minnesota enacted what is commonly known as the "No-Fault Divorce Act." This dramatic and welcome reform replaced the old concept of fault with a more practical analysis: if one party desired to end the marriage, no real marriage continued to exist. Therefore, most of the grounds for divorce were removed from the statute and the law now reads:

> A dissolution of marriage shall be granted by a county or district court when the court finds that there has been an irretrievable breakdown of the marriage relationship.

Minnesota Statutes Section 518.06 (1988).

Now, the court may rely on one of two factors as proof of an irretrievable breakdown in the marriage relationship. If the parties have lived separately for six months, or if one party testifies that there is serious marital discord affecting the attitude of one or both parties toward the marriage, a dissolution is granted. No other proof is necessary; one party's testimony that the marriage is over is sufficient to end the marriage (*Minnesota Statutes Section 518.13, subd. 2 (1988)*).

There is no defense to a divorce. Prior to 1974, if a person condoned or participated in marital misconduct, the parties could be denied a divorce. Now, if one party wants to be single again, the divorce will be granted. When the laws were changed, the term "divorce" was replaced by the term "marriage dissolution." "No-fault divorce" limits the adversarial nature of a divorce by removing the requirement for grounds and defenses. Even the caption in a dissolution does not use the accusatory labels of Plaintiff and Defendant; instead the caption reads "In Re the Marriage of the Petitioner and the Respondent." One person is asking the court for something (the Petitioner), and the other is answering (the Respondent).

The initial paperwork commencing an action for marriage dissolution is simple and resembles an informational worksheet. The petition states the names, addresses and birth dates of both parties; the date and place of marriage; whether there are children involved and, if so, their names and ages; and the existence of any real estate owned by either party. A party seeking a divorce must be a resident of the state of Minnesota for six months before beginning an action. Generally, the last paragraph of the petition asks the court to enter an order dissolving the marriage; to determine child custody, support and maintenance; and to divide the property equitably between the parties.

The simple procedure for beginning a marriage dissolution can give a false picture of the complexities involved. Marriage dissolution involves unique and emotional relationships. The issue of whether the marriage will end is simple. The consequence is that two parties are going to restructure their lives, and perhaps their children's lives, based on the fact that they will no longer be married to one another. Some couples come to a mutual understanding that they no longer wish to be married and can divide assets in an equitable manner with little participation by the courts. Other couples have special problems with property, support or custody that cannot be resolved easily, and those people look to the court to resolve them.

The laws that apply to divorce come from two sources: the statutes enacted by the legislature, and court decisions.

The dissolution statutes enacted by the legislature are generally contained in Chapter 518 of the Minnesota Statutes; however, there are dozens of other provisions which relate to the wide variety of issues involved in a divorce. Because divorce is so uniquely affected by our social and economic climate, there are constant revisions being made to these statutes. Dozens of changes have been made in the past 14 years and more are enacted each legislative session.

While the legislature enacts laws, the courts are charged with interpreting them. Every day, Minnesota courts are asked to define statutes as they apply to particular facts. While trial courts handle divorce cases every day, the particular facts of those cases and the decisions made by those judges are not published or catalogued in any one place. Further, the decision of one district court judge does not control another's. However, decisions of the Minnesota Supreme Court, which interpret a particular statute, control and direct the trial courts in their daily determinations. Because appeals to the Minnesota Supreme Court were once a relatively uncommon occurrence, divorce law was largely limited to the statutes and a small number of key cases decided by the Minnesota Supreme Court each year.

In 1983, Minnesota adopted a two-tier system of appellate review. With the establishment of the Minnesota Court of Appeals, all district court cases now have an opportunity for review. This appellate court cannot refuse to hear an appeal that is properly before it. The Minnesota Supreme Court may then review the appellate court decision if one of the parties appeals it, but the Minnesota Supreme Court selects only cases of major importance that focus on the development of the law.

Our intermediate appellate court has developed a comprehensive body of family law which was sorely needed. These decisions have produced massive changes in the interpretation and application of the statutes.

It is impossible to compress all of this new law into one small book. Instead, this book addresses some of the common issues with which people struggle in family law. Topics have been chosen which illustrate some of the most recent changes in the law and the more practical issues that face divorcing people. The simple question-and-answer format will help you understand the topics that are important to you. Even as you read this book, changes in the law may be enacted. To help keep the book's readership current and the information timely, after June 30 of each year the firm of Chestnut & Brooks will provide a brief statutory and case-law update referenced to the pages in this book.

To receive the update, simply contact Chestnut & Brooks (612/339-7300) and request the revision related to this book.

CHAPTER 1

How is the property divided in a dissolution?

When you married, you probably believed that the income and possessions of you and your spouse would always be shared, yet all of this changes when the marriage is terminated. In a marital dissolution, the courts are faced with the intricate task of sorting out the individual pieces of what was supposed to be a unified estate. This process is called classification and distribution of property.

The decisions in this process may be made by a judge in a trial, or they may be settled between the two parties if they negotiate an agreement called a stipulation, or Marital Termination Agreement (see an example of such a document later in the book). In either case, anyone involved in a dissolution should be aware of the laws that govern the determination.

When a couple marries, all of the property acquired by either party, together or separately, after the date of the marriage is presumed to be "marital property" and is subject to fair and equitable division. This property may include real estate, personal property, legal rights and vested pension benefits.

The issue examined is whether the property was acquired during the marriage, not whether it was titled to one party alone. Whether the title is held in one or both names, in joint tenancy or tenancy in common has no bearing on the classification. These types of ownership are relevant to other legal circumstances, but not to dissolution. Property or property rights that you or your spouse acquire after getting married are all presumed to be marital property.

Understanding these classifications is critical because the court divides marital property equitably in a marital dissolution. It is supposed to be divided fairly, just as if two equal owners of a business were liquidating their assets.

Some property can be classified as "non-marital" and separated from the marital estate for division. The law states that non-marital property includes the following:

a. property inherited or received as a gift by one party alone during the marriage;
b. property acquired before the marriage;
c. property acquired in exchange for non-marital property, or the increase in value of non-marital property;
d. property acquired by one party alone after a legal separation; or
e. property excluded by an antenuptial contract.

Minnesota Statutes Section 518.54, subd. 5(a-e) (1988).

Property acquired after marriage, but before divorce, is marital unless it falls into one of the above categories. For example, if one party enters the marriage with a coin collection, jewelry and some family heirlooms, it is fairly clear that those pieces of property should be returned to the party who brought them to the marriage. However, some property interests, such as real estate, businesses and stock investments, change in character and value over time. Those changes create the most tangled problems in asset classification and can cause great trauma in dissolutions when parties discover an enormous difference in what they thought they would get and what they actually receive.

In many marriage dissolutions, the homestead is often the major asset to be divided. Most homes are purchased with a downpayment and a mortgage used to finance the balance. However, the actual equity owned may be only 20 percent or less. Equity in a home increases in three ways:

1. mortgage paydown;
2. improvements; or
3. appreciation.

As a general rule, increases in equity produced by improvements or mortgage paydown during the course of the marriage will be deemed marital, while appreciation will be apportioned according to a formula called the *Schmitz* formula. The law requires that the court examine the reason for the increase in value and make its classification based on the source of the increase.

For example, if John bought a house for $100,000 by putting $20,000 down, his equity would be 20% of the house's market value, or $20,000. Assume that John marries Jane and their marriage lasts for three years. During that time they make no improvements to the property, but due to rapid appreciation it doubles in value. Since very little mortgage paydown would have occurred in those three years, the entire increase in value could be attributed to inflation. If the home were sold for $200,000, approximately $80,000 would pay the mortgage balance, $40,000 would be given to John as his doubled non-marital interest, and the remaining $80,000 would be divided equally between John and Jane as marital property.

If the property's value had not increased due to appreciation, but was caused by improvements that John and Jane made during their three years together, then John's non-marital interest would remain $20,000 and the entire increase in equity would constitute marital property.

Assume instead that the two were married for 30 years and, for some reason, the house never appreciated in value but the mortgage was paid off. Then John's non-marital interest would be $20,000 and the $80,000 mortgage paydown would constitute marital property to be divided equally in a dissolution.

The history of home ownership is seldom that simple, especially over a long period of time. Additions can be built, homes can be refinanced, or they can sustain damage or decrease in value. However, the above analysis is a starting point for defining the various parts of a home's value as marital and non-marital property.

While homes may be difficult to classify, businesses can be even trickier. The value of a business, unlike a home, is measured in terms of intangibles, such as effort, "goodwill" value and anticipated future sales. This will be discussed in more detail in the next chapter.

Business assets can change dramatically over time. Let us assume that Roxanne owned ten high-rise construction cranes which she leased to construction companies. She married Jerry when the company was worth one million dollars. Their marriage lasted for seven years. If, at the time of the divorce, Roxanne still owned the same ten cranes and the company was still worth one million dollars, then classification is an easy task. There is no increased value in what was clearly a non-marital asset. All business assets belong to Roxanne. Even if, using the same example, inflation had increased the value of the business by 50%, still no part of the company becomes marital property.

If, however, during the course of the marriage, the parties had doubled the number of cranes owned by the company, then half of the present value of the company would be classified as marital property, and the other half would remain non-marital.

These examples deal only with tangible business assets. In a recent case, *Nardini v. Nardini,* the Minnesota Supreme Court tried to untangle the division of marital and non-marital business property in a divorce. In 1949, before he married, the husband spent $2,500 to buy half the interest in the business where he worked. Four years later, in 1953, he married, and a few years after that the couple bought out the remaining partner. During their 30-year marriage, the two worked together to run their home, raise their children and develop their business. When they decided to divorce, the books and records of the corporation showed the business assets to be worth $500,000.

The husband argued that because he had bought half of the original partnership *before* he was married, half of the current $500,000 value should be returned directly to him as non-marital property. Then, the remaining $250,000 should be divided between him and his wife, giving the wife only one fourth of the business' value.

The wife argued that the original $2,500 payment was inconsequential. She claimed the real increase in the business value resulted from their 30 years of hard work and reinvesting their profits. The trial judge agreed with the husband and gave him half of the business "off the top." However, the Minnesota Supreme Court disagreed.

The Court accepted this case for review because it was unfair to call half of this major asset non-marital property. It held that the increase in value was not merely the result of inflation, but the result of both parties' hard work and reinvestment. The court therefore determined that the business was almost exclusively a marital asset, to be divided by both.

The law *presumes* that all the property owned by a married couple is marital property to be equally divided, and imposes on the party who wants the property classified as non-marital the burden of proving that it is non-marital.

Commingling of marital and non-marital assets can cause the non-marital asset to lose its separate identity, as can a clear intent, demonstrated by the parties' actions, to treat the asset as marital property. For example, if one spouse inherited $10,000 and kept the money in a separate fund, it would retain its non-marital character.

However, if that same money were deposited in the parties' joint account and used by both over a period of years, its non-marital character would be destroyed. But there is an exception to this rule. If the claiming party can trace the asset to its origin, then it can retain its non-marital character. For example, if the $10,000 were placed in a joint account and shortly thereafter an asset costing $10,000 were purchased "with Grandma's funds," then the tracing requirement can be met and the asset would retain its non-marital character. Circumstances connecting funds to a specific purchase are not always that obvious, and the passage of time naturally weakens the link between the transactions.

The law also recognizes that up to one-half of the property classified as non-marital can be put back into the marital estate for division if doing otherwise would create a major hardship for the person without the interest. This "hardship" showing is not easily met. The distribution must create an overwhelming financial burden for the other party.

Under these rules, it is difficult to achieve total fairness. For example, if before Jane and John got married they each had $10,000 to use for joint expenditures, *what* each person spends the money on will determine who gets a non-marital interest that may be returned to them if they divorce. Presume that Jane uses her $10,000 as the downpayment on their home, and John uses his to pay for the wedding, the honeymoon and some furniture. Twenty years later, if they divorce, Jane gets her $10,000 back, along with its appreciation in the value of the house. John's money is simply spent, and the furniture is now many years old. Strict application of the law does not always provide a fair solution, so each fact situation requires careful analysis.

These rules for property division do not apply to people who are simply living together, nor do they cover the time that a couple spends living together before they marry. However, if two people live together in a purported marriage which is later annulled, these rules do apply to them.

CHAPTER 2

My spouse is self-employed and the sole owner of his business, which he started after we were married. How is the value of the business decided?

When valuing a business, documents which show its history of profit and loss, salaries paid, and the fair market value of tangible assets are critical. It is not unusual to employ a specialized business appraiser to examine the books and physical assets. Sometimes the physical assets, such as office furniture and equipment, are not the main measure of a business' worth. For example, a service business, such as a sales representative's, will have few physical assets. The real value of the business is its established track record and its ability to earn income, which can be predicted into the future. This ability to earn income and to be an ongoing concern far into the future is called "goodwill" value, and this value can be assessed.

Accountants and appraisers can take very different views of the physical assets of a business. One might value the business as if all its assets were being sold piecemeal in a sort of "fire sale" approach. Another may look at the value of the hard goods as they are carried on the books for tax purposes. This method generally reflects what it cost to acquire these goods, less depreciation according to tax tables.

In a divorce, physical division of a business is seldom a realistic option, because ex-spouses seldom make good future business partners. Often, only one spouse has been actively involved in the daily business, and that person usually wants to be awarded the whole business in order to maintain his or her job.

Some courts have said that the spouse who is not going to retain ownership of the business really owns a minority, or non-controlling, interest in that business. Generally, a non-controlling interest in a business is worth less than the same percentage of the business as a whole. Such discounts in valuing a non-controlling share are correctly applied to estates or business partnerships. However, in the recent case of *Nardini v. Nardini* (discussed in the previous chapter), the Supreme Court rejected such an artificial discount as inapplicable in a divorce where one party is receiving the entire business as an operating entity without any changes or interruption in the business. The court held that valuation of the business should be calculated as if the entire business were changing hands between a willing buyer and a willing seller. If this is the standard, then goodwill and the business' history, along with its tangible assets, must be valued. According to the *Nardini* decision, a company can never be valued at less than the value of its assets if sold in a piecemeal fashion, and even a "liquidation" or "fire sale" value may be totally unrealistic if the entire entity is being awarded to one party.

We still have a variety of accounting principles to apply to the value of a business, but the court gives us direction as to which theory of valuation can be applied.

Certain "business-style" assets that belong to one party alone cannot be valued as part of the business. For example, a physician who operates a private practice in partnership has not only a business interest, but also his or her medical degree and license. The business partnership, its physical assets, its accounts receivable and its track record must all be evaluated in the divorce. However, one spouse's ongoing ability to practice a profession by virtue of a degree and license is not something that is evaluated and divided in the Minnesota state courts. In other states, courts have recognized that professional licenses give a person the ability to earn a higher income than that person would earn without the professional license or degree. In Minnesota, the non-professional spouse's interest in that degree is limited. A supporting spouse who helps the other earn a degree or license by providing financial support can recover that contribution. However, future earnings from that license cannot be counted as part of the value of the business and cannot be divided in the divorce as part of the marital estate.

It is very important, if you have a business and are involved in a divorce, that you retain competent professionals to acquire all of the information necessary to make a sound evaluation and determine the best way to value and divide your marital estate.

CHAPTER 3

Are pensions assets to be divided in a dissolution?

By the year Two Thousand, 599,959 people, or 13% of Minnesota's population, will be over the age of 65. This statistic comes from Minnesota's State Office of Demographics. As the baby-boomers reach retirement, aging and all of its attendant concerns will be relevant to a greater portion of the population. Today, if you reach age 65, your chances of a longer life increase; therefore, you will be dependent on your pension income for a longer period of time than your predecessors.

The financial needs of retirees are a growing societal concern. Pension plans have consequently increased in importance as the divorce rate grows and the number of elderly increases. In many middle-aged households there may be only two major assets: the homestead and the pension rights. Pension plans are marital property and, upon dissolution, the court will make an equitable division of those pension benefits which were accumulated during a marriage.

There are basically two kinds of retirement plans: the defined contribution plan and the defined benefit plan. In a defined contribution plan, the employer makes specific contributions and the employee may be permitted or required to contribute as well. Each participant has an individual account, making it easy to administer. Valuing such a plan simply requires reviewing the most recent account statement of the participant.

Defined benefit plans are more complex because the benefits are derived from a combination of factors: highest income levels of the participant, retirement age and number of employment years. Because an employer's contributions are not necessarily fixed, and individual accounts are not maintained, determining the value of such a pension plan is more difficult.

It is important to remember that benefits which are earned before a marriage are not marital property. For example, if your husband was employed by an airline for ten years before your 20-year marriage, and has a pension with a present value of $90,000, then one-third of those pension benefits are subject to a non-marital claim. This is the formula that the court uses to calculate the division of a pension:

> The marital interest in each payment will be the fraction of that payment, the numerator of the fraction being the number of years (or months) of marriage during which benefits were being accumulated; the denominator being the total number of years (or months) during which benefits were accumulated prior to when paid. The non-employee spouse will receive a percentage of the marital interest in each payment.

Applied to the above set of facts, the formula looks like this:

1. $Y = \frac{90{,}000 \times 20}{30}$

2. $Y = \frac{180{,}000}{30}$

3. $Y = 60{,}000$

If the pension is worth $90,000 at dissolution, then $30,000 of the pension fund is non-marital and belongs to the husband who earned it when single. The remaining $60,000 is a marital asset which, if equally divided, yields $30,000 to the wife and $30,000 to the husband. Therefore, of the total pension, the wife will receive $30,000 and the husband will receive $60,000 ($30,000 marital funds and $30,000 non-marital funds).

Experts may arrive at completely different values for the same pension fund, because there are two methods of valuing pensions: the fixed-percentage method and the present-value method.

Using the fixed-percentage method, the court applies a formula for division of the pension at the time of dissolution. Then the beneficiary is awarded that percentage when and if the participant begins to receive benefits. Therefore, the actual division of the asset is postponed until retirement occurs.

Under the present-value method, other assets of equivalent value are awarded to the non-participant spouse. To determine present value, the court calculates the percentage of marital interests along with such factors as vesting, maturity and the participant's mortality. Half of that sum is awarded to the spouse in a lump sum of property of equivalent value if 100% of the pension was accumulated during the marriage.

For example, if a pension's present marital value equaled $100,000, then $50,000 would be due the spouse (alternative payee). If the homestead had equity of $120,000, each party's share of the property would be $60,000.

If a wife wished to keep the homestead, instead of paying her husband his $60,000 share, she might trade her $50,000 pension share and pay him $10,000 in cash. In that way, she would be awarded the house, and her husband would be awarded his full pension benefits.

Because it has the advantage of finality, the court prefers the present-value method of distribution and will use it when the parties have sufficient assets to accommodate such a split and will not suffer undue hardship. There is a complete severing of the parties' interests, unlike the fixed-percentage method which requires the court's continued involvement.

Until recently, the date of the separation or of the divorce decree was the date used for marital asset determination. However, as of 1988, the day the dissolution is filed is the date used to determine valuation of all marital assets. This is a new rule and will no doubt be applied to pension valuation as well.

An emerging area of the law in Minnesota examines the dual characteristics attributed to divided pensions which are coupled with permanent maintenance awards. Simply put, if a pension is valued and split either by the court or by stipulation, can those same pension dollars later be considered income when the participant retires?

At retirement, a maintenance payor frequently moves the court either for reduction or cessation of a permanent maintenance award. Because a person's income usually decreases at retirement, the event is an opportunity to show "changed circumstances" which meet the modification standard. Only one Minnesota Appeals Court case in 1988 addressed this issue; however, it was an unusual case and more litigation should clarify the law in the coming year.

As of 1984, special rules were designed to provide for the distribution of pension benefits in a divorce action. These rules are a combination of state and federal laws and they govern the issuance of a Qualified Domestic Relations Order (QDRO). A QDRO is a device for dividing the benefits in a variety of pension plans:

1. defined benefit plans;
2. defined contribution plans;
3. profit sharing plans;
4. stock bonus plans;
5. employee stock-ownership plans;
6. money-purchased pension plans (ESOPs); and
7. target benefit pension plans.

Because of the complexity of this area of the law, experts are often hired to draft the QDRO needed to divide the benefits upon dissolution. There are specific limits and requirements on the form a QDRO may take; errors can prevent an order from "qualifying."

Finally, it is appropriate to include just a few words about Social Security benefits. Social Security benefits earned in the marriage are not divisible at divorce as are other pension benefits. If a husband has pension benefits and a wife has only Social Security benefits, the wife gets part of her husband's pension at divorce, but the husband does not get part of his wife's Social Security benefits.

Whether or not a wife was employed during her marriage does not determine her eligibility for Social Security benefits. If she was married for at least ten years, then she is entitled to derivative benefits from her husband's Social Security contributions.

If she does not remarry by age 62, she can receive retirement or disability benefits. If her husband receives benefits and she is not yet age 62 and has been divorced for at least two years, she can receive benefits.

If a woman remarries after age 60, she can continue to receive derivative benefits from her former husband's Social Security or choose to take benefits under her new husband's Social Security, depending upon which is larger.

Contact your Social Security office for specific details in your circumstances. You should also obtain from your local Social Security Administration office two copies of Form SSA-7004, the Personal Earnings and Benefits Statement. If you have worked, your first request should be for your own earnings and the second for those of your former spouse. In that way, you'll be sure that all benefits have been credited to your account.

CHAPTER 4

If I get a divorce, will I (or my spouse) be ordered to pay spousal maintenance?

Spousal maintenance, the term now used instead of "alimony," is the monthly support payment that one spouse pays to another. Whether someone pays or receives maintenance depends on many factors, which will be discussed in greater detail later in this chapter.

The evolution of Minnesota divorce law shows that the reasons for granting a maintenance award have shifted with the changing times. In the late 1800s, the courts could be hard on a divorcing woman. If a woman deserted her husband or committed adultery, she was given no separate alimony, or maintenance. The court's focus was on who committed the "wrong." For example, if a wife could prove that her husband had committed adultery, she might be awarded maintenance. Back then, no one examined *what* each party contributed to a marriage; this is a modern concept.

In the 1930s, Minnesota courts repeatedly held that the husband had a long-term duty to support his wife. But it was not until 1955 that adultery was removed as a bar to receiving maintenance. Until 1969, maintenance could be awarded only to women. Then the legislature stated that maintenance could be payable to a "spouse," not only to a wife.

With the onset of "no-fault" divorce in the 1970s, the legislature and the courts struggled to keep stride with the changing societal norms which were rapidly evolving. Women were no longer regarded as helpless individuals in need of protection. Instead, through the women's movement, a new image evolved portraying women as equal partners to men, capable of providing for their own support.

In 1972, however, a Florida court took this concept to the extreme, with disastrous results for a 48-year-old wife exiting a long-term marriage. Her award of permanent maintenance was overturned and replaced with two years of rehabilitative maintenance. The court reasoned that she could equip herself, through education or training, to provide for her own needs. The court had a "modern," though inaccurate, view of societal expectations for a woman leaving a long-term marriage.

Today, some of the reasons a court might award maintenance may include any or all of these:

1. to honor a sense of duty;
2. to keep the dependent spouse off public assistance;
3. to minimize financial disruption caused by divorce;
4. to compensate for lost opportunity; or
5. to rehabilitate a spouse absent from the job market.

Maintenance may be characterized in several ways: rehabilitative, temporary or permanent. The idea of compensation for lost opportunity gave birth to rehabilitative maintenance, which allows a dependent spouse, presumably disadvantaged by years of homemaking, time to retrain for entry into the workforce.

Temporary maintenance is given when the court finds that training, education, or a period of on-the-job experience is required before a party's income is likely to rise to the point of self-sufficiency. Defining this period involves some speculation, and each case is governed by its own facts. If the spouse seeking maintenance has a definite educational plan, then evidence from schools, training programs, or vocational counselors can be introduced to help the court determine the amount of time needed to train and acquire employment.

In 1985, permanent maintenance awards were given a new characterization; before that change, courts were hesitant to award permanent maintenance. According to the statute, if there is any uncertainty about the need for permanent spousal maintenance, a permanent award should be given over a temporary one.

The *Nardini* case, mentioned earlier in this book, contains a clear statement about the award of permanent maintenance.

There, our supreme court reversed a trial court judge's decision to limit maintenance and held that in the case of a long-term, traditional marriage such as the Nardinis', maintenance should be awarded on a permanent basis. The court said it was irrelevant that the trial court had reserved jurisdiction to review the temporary award in the future. Considering the wife's employment history and age, the uncertainty over the need for permanent maintenance required the court to make a permanent award. Of course, the award is subject to future modification upon motion by the husband, but only if he can prove a substantial change of circumstances.

In order to qualify for *any* maintenance award, a party must satisfy at least one of three criteria showing that the dependent spouse:

1. lacks sufficient property to meet his or her reasonable needs; or
2. is unable to provide adequate self-support through employment, considering the standard of living established during the marriage; or
3. is the custodian of a child whose condition requires that the spouse not seek employment outside the home.

Minnesota Statutes Section 518.552, subd. 1 (1988).

The court will require the parties to submit detailed income and expense documentation showing that a financial imbalance exists between them.

The Minnesota Statutes list the factors the court must consider in determining the amount and duration of any maintenance award:

> Subd. 2. The maintenance order shall be in amounts and for periods of time, either temporary or permanent, as the court deems just, without regard to marital misconduct, and after considering all relevant factors, including:

a. the financial resources of the party seeking maintenance, including marital property apportioned to the party, and the party's ability to meet needs independently, including the extent to which a provision for support of a child living with the party includes a sum for that party as custodian;
b. the time necessary to acquire sufficient education or training to enable the party seeking maintenance to find appropriate employment, and the probability, given the party's age and skills, of completing education or training and becoming fully or partially self-supporting;
c. the standard of living established during the marriage;
d. the duration of the marriage and, in the case of a homemaker, the length of absence from employment and the extent to which any education, skills or experience have become outmoded and earning capacity has become permanently denied;
e. the loss of earnings, seniority, retirement benefits and other employment opportunities forgone by the spouse seeking spousal maintenance;
f. the age, and the physical and emotional condition of the spouse seeking maintenance;
g. the ability of the spouse from whom maintenance is sought to meet needs while meeting those of the spouse seeking maintenance; and
h. the contribution of each party in the acquisition, preservation, depreciation, or appreciation in the amount or value of the marital property, as well as the contribution of a spouse as a homemaker or in furtherance of the other party's employment or business.

Minnesota Statutes Section 518.552, subd. 2(a-h) (1988).

While the court is instructed to consider each of these factors, there is no direction on the weight to be given any one factor.

To determine the parties' income for purposes of setting maintenance, the court examines sources beyond just wages or salary. If one party in the divorce is awarded investment property, stocks that pay dividends, or a substantial cash award that can earn interest, the income value of these awards will be used to determine whether that party will be able to meet future needs. If the court decides that one party is unlikely to be immediately self-supporting, then the court must determine a level of support and the length of time it should be paid.

The court will examine the possibility of rehabilitating the dependent spouse to re-enter the job market. Such a plan must be feasible, unlike the Florida decision which gave the wife only two years to return to full employment. The Minnesota Statutes use the term "appropriate" employment. Forty-eight-year old people do not usually begin medical school and, conversely, clerking in a dime store does not equate to appropriate employment for a college-educated person.

Lifestyle should be taken into account by the court. The statute provides that the court consider "the standard of living established during the marriage." Although the court may indeed attempt to do that, much work still needs to be done in that area. A recent California study revealed some startling, now famous statistics: on the average, divorced women experienced a 73% decline in their standard of living, whereas their husbands experienced a 42% increase. The No-Fault Divorce Act has created a new class of financially desperate citizens labeled the "underclass."

The court also considers the duration of the marriage. Naturally, the longer the marriage the better one party's chance of receiving a permanent spousal maintenance award. If one party has been a traditional homemaker during a long-term marriage, the fact that the party has been removed from the job market for an extended time will weigh in favor of permanent and higher maintenance. The court also considers a homemaker's loss of opportunity to accrue earnings, seniority, retirement and other employment benefits. Long-time absence from the job market is viewed by the court as an impairment.

The physical and emotional condition of the dependent spouse is examined by the court; so if a party suffers from any health problems, these should be documented to the court in the form of a doctor's written opinion.

On the basis of all this information, the court will make its determination regarding maintenance: 1) whether it will be awarded, and 2) if so, the amount and duration of the award.

If you and your spouse agree on the terms of your settlement and draft a stipulation, or Marital Termination Agreement, be sure that you include in that document a provision requiring adequate life insurance coverage on your spouse. To determine the amount of coverage needed, estimate the total maintenance (and child support) that would be paid over the term of years. The overall insurance coverage should equal the estimated amount. For an example of such a provision, see item #20 in the sample Marital Termination Agreement included later in this book.

CHAPTER 5

How can a maintenance award be changed?

Awards of either temporary or permanent maintenance can be modified. If the original award was a temporary one, a party may extend the date for its termination. The party receiving the maintenance must make a motion to the court to change the duration of maintenance before the order comes to its natural end.

The courts have the power to amend spousal maintenance awards, in either amount or duration, so long as maintenance is still payable at the time the modification is requested. If the period for temporary spousal maintenance has passed and it is no longer payable, the court will no longer have jurisdiction over the order.

Sometimes temporary spousal maintenance awards are written so that payments are made over a certain period of time, then cease. However, "jurisdiction" may be reserved for an additional period of time. In that case, the original order may be reopened for modification. Further maintenance payments may be reinstituted if circumstances have substantially changed requiring continuation of maintenance.

If permanent spousal maintenance was given in the original award, either party may petition the court for a change, so long as maintenance is still payable.

A maintenance award may be modified upon a showing of one or more of the following:

1. substantially increased or decreased earnings of a party;
2. substantially increased or decreased needs of a party;
3. receipt of public assistance; or
4. a change in the cost of living for either party.

Minnesota Statutes Section 518.64, subd. 2 (1988).

The party requesting the modification must demonstrate two things: a substantial change of circumstances, and the unfairness of the existing obligation as a result of the change. Clear proof is required, and the burden of proof is on the party requesting the change. If the court decides that a substantial change has occurred, then it must apply the factors in Section 518.552 and determine the amount of either the increase or reduction.

A word of caution: maintenance awards are only reluctantly altered. One Minnesota case shows that a 12% decrease in the payor's income was significant, but not sufficiently substantial to be called a change of circumstances. No reduction was granted. Likewise, an increase in the payor's income is not, on its own, a substantial change of circumstances.

The important thing to remember is that the party requesting the change has the burden of proof, and along with that goes the responsibility to present adequate documentation to the court.

However, if the court either fails to award or fails to reserve jurisdiction to award maintenance at a future time, maintenance cannot be awarded later. Previous cases have shown that if a decree fails specifically to reserve the issue of maintenance for future determination, jurisdiction cannot be claimed subsequently.

In early 1989, the Minnesota Supreme Court declared that an order based on a stipulation which expressly waives the right to modify maintenance cannot be reopened. The *Karon* case was hotly disputed. In that case, the original stipulation provided for $1,200 in monthly spousal maintenance for six years and $600 per month for four years thereafter. The stipulation contained the following language:

> Except for the aforesaid maintenance, each party waives and is forever barred from receiving any spousal maintenance whatsoever from one another, and this court is divested from having any jurisdiction whatsoever to

award temporary or permanent spousal maintenance to either of the parties.

Four years into this agreement, the wife moved for a maintenance modification, requesting an increase to $3,500 per month. The trial court awarded her $1,500 in permanent monthly maintenance and the award was affirmed by the Court of Appeals. But the Minnesota Supreme Court overturned the award, claiming that changing the contract was insulting and demeaning to women. The Court said it would not protect women from their own decisions if they were represented by competent counsel because women are not children in need of such supervision. Three of the judges disagreed and two wrote dissents. More litigation may follow from this case.

The *Karon* case demonstrates that you must be very careful when you draft your stipulation. If the terms of your stipulation state an absolute ending date to maintenance and the stipulation waives jurisdiction, it cannot later be changed without a showing of fraud.

CHAPTER 6

What factors affect my right to custody?

The litigation process is not a neutral one. In it, courts attempt to sort out the rights and obligations of parties by measuring the law and the facts to produce a fair result. In family law, the measurements are different, because this litigation involves economic and emotional issues, and none are more deeply felt than those surrounding child custody.

Children suffer in divorce in a variety of ways. Their relationships with other children suffer; their ties to the community may be altered, and the resulting insecurity may affect their ability to function in school and at home.

A custody battle attempts to sort out pre-existing rights of parents, but the very process is inherently destructive to the children at issue in the battle.

Dry as definitions may be, they are helpful in understanding some of the terms to be used in this chapter.

Legal Custody means having the right to determine the child's upbringing, including education, health care and religious training.

Joint Legal Custody means that both parents have equal rights and responsibilities, including the right to participate in major decisions determining the child's upbringing, including education, health care and religious training.

Physical Custody designates who provides the routine daily care, control and residence of the child.

Joint Physical Custody means that the routine daily care, control and residence of the child are shared by both parents.

Custodial Parent, or ***Custodian,*** means the person who has physical custody of the child at any particular time.

The court may grant one person sole custody of a child or establish joint custody. There is a presumption for joint legal custody. If sole custody is granted, then the custodial parent has the sole authority to make all major decisions about the child's upbringing, including education, religion, discipline and medical treatment.

Today, men may claim that courts still favor women in custody issues and operate on the presumption that a young child is best cared for by its mother. Yet, that concept is 180 degrees from antiquated English common law, which regarded children as chattel over whom the father had complete control. That same man had complete control over his wife. Before the turn of the century, women had few rights under the law, even regarding their own children. Minnesota law formerly gave preference to paternal custody.

By the 1920s, the court's attitude had evolved full circle and began to favor women as the caretakers for young children. The "tender years doctrine" reigned for more than 30 years: courts repeatedly held that children of tender years were best served by a mother's care.

By the 1970s, this kind of thinking came under attack. The movie "Kramer v. Kramer" raised the public's consciousness by challenging the sexual stereotypes which favored maternal custody. So too, in Minnesota courts, proponents of equality claimed that the best interests of the child were obscured by the court's maternal preference, resulting in unfair discrimination against men.

By 1969, Minnesota had adopted the "best interests of the child" standard to be applied in custody decisions. It was hoped that the standard would remove sexism from the court's decisions. From 1969 to 1974, the legislature directed the courts to consider a child's age and sex when determining custody. For example, girls were thought to be best raised by "moms," and older boys needed their "dads." With this test, the trial courts made a case-by-case analysis of each custody dispute. Unfortunately, it was an imperfect system which resulted in some horrible inequities.

The sex-neutral test, which focused on the best interests of the child, had the unhappy and unexpected result of increasing the father's bargaining power while reducing the mother's. By removing the assurance that a mother would prevail in a serious custody dispute, a mother's natural fear of losing her child colored her decisions in settlement negotiations. A father could use the threat of a custody battle to obtain financial concessions resulting from her fears. Lower maintenance and lower child support settlements resulted, as items exchanged for a dropped custody dispute.

These events operated on the theory that the father's bottom line was saving money and the mother's was keeping the children. Times have changed, as has the arsenal of weaponry used to rebut those presumptions. However, such concepts historically played a strong role in dissolution decisions.

Subsequently, however, a bitter Minnesota custody battle produced a new standard. In *Pikula v. Pikula,* the court held that when both parents seek custody of a child too young to express a parental preference, custody should be given to the "primary" parent, absent a showing that the primary parent is unfit.

To determine which parent was the primary caretaker, the court listed ten factors to be considered;

1. preparing and planning meals;
2. bathing, grooming and dressing;
3. purchasing, cleaning, and care of clothes;
4. medical care, including nursing and trips to physicians;
5. arranging for social interaction among peers after school (for example, transporting to friends' houses);
6. arranging alternative care (babysitting, daycare, putting the child to bed at night, attending the child in the night, waking the child in the morning);
7. educating;
8. disciplining (teaching general manners and toilet training);
9. religious training; and
10. teaching elementary skills.

By adopting this primary-caretaker test, Minnesota attempted to remove the existing inequities in child custody decisions. By removing financial bargaining power from the non-custodial parent, and by avoiding sexual stereotypes and preferences, it was hoped the best interests of the child would be served. Either parent could be granted custody under this test, which also recognized a child's need for continuity in parenting.

The *Pikula* test is not applied if a parent is unfit. It is to be applied as of the date of separation, if the separation is reasonably close in time to the hearing date. In situations where neither parent is the primary caretaker, or the child is old enough to express a preference, then the best-interests test should be applied, along with application of the *Pikula* test.

The criteria provided by current law are found in *Minnesota Statutes 518.155-185.* They include:

a. the wishes of the child's parent or parents as to his custody;
b. the reasonable preference of the child, if the court deems the child to be of sufficient age to express a preference;
c. the interaction and interrelationship of the child with its parents, its siblings, and any other person who is significant to the child's best interests;
d. the child's adjustment to his home, school, and community;
e. the length of time the child has lived in a stable, satisfactory environment and the desirability of maintaining continuity;
f. the performance, as a family unit, of the existing or proposed custodial home;
g. the mental and physical health of the individuals involved;
h. the capacity and disposition of the parties to give the child love, affection and guidance, and to continue educating and raising the child in his culture and religion or creed, if any;
i. the child's cultural background; and
j. the effect of abuse on the child, if domestic abuse, as defined in Section 518B.01, has occurred.

If parents seek either joint legal or joint physical custody, a court must consider the following additional factors:

a. the ability of the parents to cooperate in the rearing of their children;
b. methods for resolving disputes regarding any major decision concerning the life of the child, and the parents' willingness to use those methods; and
c. whether it would be detrimental to the child if one parent were to have sole authority of the child's upbringing.

Custody is an emotionally charged issue. Many divorcing couples lack the emotional maturity needed to solve such matters. Once the relationship is dead, the parties' ability to function as partners often dissolves.

Court Services exists to fill this need by offering counseling, mediation and evaluation services to assist in family court matters. Court Services employs counselors who assist people in mediating disputes that arise in divorce, primarily relating to children.

The counselor first interviews both parties and then tries to help a family develop a custody and visitation plan that is acceptable to both parties and is in the best interests of the children. If no agreement can be reached, it is the counselor's responsibility to prepare a report detailing all relevant facts regarding both parties and the children. Generally, the court will set a date for this report to be submitted. Another court date will be scheduled for some time after the report is to be submitted, in order to allow the parties and their attorneys to evaluate the completeness and accuracy of the report and to comment to the court on it. While the court puts great weight on these reports, they are not binding on the judge. Supplementary information is usually helpful either to contest parts of the report or to highlight favorable segments.

Court Services investigates a broad scope of factors and requires access to all relevant information. Parents are asked to execute informational releases relative to employers, medical treatment and the like.

If the parties cannot agree even after the Court Services report is delivered, hearings can be held so that witnesses can testify and be cross-examined. The law permits children to be interviewed by the judge. This interview is usually done informally in the judge's chambers, rather than in the open courtroom; however, both parties' lawyers may be present during the interview. The judge may request input from the attorneys regarding questions to ask the child, or the judge may allow the attorneys to ask the child questions directly.

A "guardian ad litem" may be appointed for a child. A guardian ad litem is a person charged with representing the child's best interests. This person is often an attorney, but the law does not require this. It requires a neutral person, unrelated to either parent or their attorneys. The appointment of a guardian ad litem is usually limited to complex or hotly disputed cases, or cases where children have special needs that may not currently be met by either party. Either parent, or the court, may request appointment of a guardian ad litem to speak directly for a child.

Minnesota Statutes Section 260.155, subd. 4a (1988) "requires that the trial court appoint a guardian ad litem in every proceeding involving neglect or dependency of a minor child. The only apparent limitation on the court's discretion is that the person selected as the guardian act in the best interests of the child to protect his rights."

A guardian ad litem may be used both in juvenile or family courts and may have a variety of duties:

1. to investigate the case;
2. to participate in negotiations and hearings;
3. to develop dispositional recommendations;
4. to present information to the court;
5. to recommend disposition to the court;
6. to have regular contact with the child;
7. to protect the child's rights;

8. to participate in decision making meetings that affect the child;
9. to monitor the case;
10. to advocate on behalf of the child;
11. to ensure that needs of the child are met;.
12. to ensure compliance with statutory requirements;
13. to examine the case
14. to determine the child's rights; or
15. to determine what defenses may exist and may be interposed with reasonable prospect of success.

Custody hearings are trials in the true sense of the word, with live witnesses called and cross-examined, but the court may exclude the public from these hearings. In a custody hearing, the court may make a variety of restrictive rulings to protect the best interests of the child. These might include confidentiality of certain interviews, reports or other information presented to the court.

Because the care of children is unique to every family, it is best to work with your spouse to find a meaningful way to share your children and to avoid the emotional stress and high cost of custody litigation. Money better used to ease the transition from joint to separate households can be consumed by attorney and court fees. Courts do not look kindly upon parents who cannot cooperate for the sake of their children.

CHAPTER 7

How much child support should each party pay?

A parental obligation to provide financial support for minor children is universally recognized. Historically, the obligation had moral overtones and was linked only to the father. Today, most jurisdictions hold both the mother and father financially responsible for minor children, and their obligations are viewed as equal in the eyes of the law.

Child support, like any other item in a dissolution, can be agreed to and included in a stipulation created outside of the court. However, a stipulation for zero child support is unenforceable because the court will not approve such an agreement. Neither party can waive child support. If agreement cannot be reached, the court will determine the amount of child support a parent must pay. To make this determination, the court will look to the child support guidelines. The guidelines were first developed as non-binding support levels to be used by social service agencies in setting the amount of child support that someone should repay the agency if the child is the recipient of public assistance. These payments served as partial reimbursement for the aid received by the child.

The guidelines were drafted in response to federal legislation which required that each state's child support enforcement agency develop such a formula. States that did not comply risked losing federal funds.

Since 1983, Minnesota Statutes have included a grid which calculates the percentage of net income applicable to the payment of child support. The grid shows a sliding scale of child support payments which are based on the amount of net income and the number of children in need of support. If the person obligated to pay support has a net monthly income of $400 or less, the guidelines do not apply. However, if the court finds that a party has intentionally decreased income to this level, it may apply the guidelines to the amount it determines the party is capable of earning.

Before these guidelines were incorporated into the Minnesota statute, it was not uncommon for lawyers to use the public assistance standards to compute reasonable child support. Child support awards were generally lower then, and support was simply doubled for a second child. If two hundred dollars was awarded for the first child, four hundred dollars was allotted for two children. As each child reached the age of majority or became emancipated, the support was decreased by the same ratio. If there were two children, the support was halved; if there were three, support was reduced by one third.

The child support guidelines do not use this ratio; instead, a smaller increase is granted for each additional child in one family. If the party earns a net monthly income of $1,000, child support for one child would be $250, for two children $300, and for three children $350. As each child reaches the age of majority, a more reasonable decrease occurs by applying this method.

For the purposes of the child support guidelines, income is defined as any form of periodic payment, including, but not limited to: wages, salaries, payments from independent contractors, and payments resulting from stipulated property settlements. Overtime is considered income if it has been a regular and steady source of income in previous years, and so are tax refunds.

Some specific items are not considered income. For example, welfare benefits are not income. This includes all forms of welfare benefits such as daycare, grants, reduced rent, AFDC, food stamps, etc. Earnings of a new spouse are not to be used to calculate a child support obligation.

Courts will examine both income and an individual's earning capacity. The court is aware that self-employed people can support themselves while reporting negligible income. In those cases, the court will look beyond earnings and examine capacity, thereby disregarding any voluntary inability to make child support payments. A party who refuses full-time employment will be regarded by the court as fully employed and will be assessed accordingly.

Originally, the guidelines were applied to the first $6,000 of net monthly income. However, subsequent amendments now limit the application of the guidelines to the first $4,000 of net monthly income.

CHILD SUPPORT GUIDELINES

The court shall multiply the obligor's net income by the percentage indicated by the following guidelines:

Net Income per Month of Obligor	Number of Children						
	1	2	3	4	5	6	7 or more
$400 and Below	Order based on the ability of the obligor to provide support at these income levels, or at higher levels, if the obligor has the earning ability.						
$401–500	14%	17%	20%	22%	24%	26%	28%
$501–550	15%	18%	21%	24%	26%	28%	30%
$551–600	16%	19%	22%	25%	28%	30%	32%
$601–650	17%	21%	24%	27%	29%	32%	34%
$651–700	18%	22%	25%	28%	31%	34%	36%
$701–750	19%	23%	27%	30%	33%	36%	38%
$751–800	20%	24%	28%	31%	35%	38%	40%
$801–850	21%	25%	29%	33%	36%	40%	42%
$851–900	22%	27%	31%	34%	38%	41%	44%
$901–950	23%	28%	32%	36%	40%	43%	46%
$951–1000	24%	29%	34%	38%	41%	45%	48%
$1001–4000	25%	30%	35%	39%	43%	47%	50%

Guidelines for support for an obligor with a monthly income of $4001 or more shall be the same dollar amounts as provided for in the guidelines for an obligor with a monthly income of $4000.

To interpret the guidelines, one must understand the definition of net monthly income. It is defined in the statute as total monthly income minus:

1. federal income tax (tax tables generally);
2. state income tax;
3. Social Security deductions;

4. reasonable pension deductions;
5. union dues;
6. cost of dependant insurance coverage;
7. cost of individual health/hospitalization or actual medical expenses; and
8. prior child support or maintenance order that is currently being paid.

Minnesota Statutes Section 518.551, subd. 5 (1988).

There have been several recent amendments to this deduction list. In the past, only mandatory pension deductions were allowed as an offset to gross income; it was later changed to allow for the deduction of "reasonable" pension payments. Because this statute is new, there is no case law defining the difference between "reasonable" and "mandatory" pension deductions. Mandatory pension deductions are those which your employer requires you to pay and that you have no right to avoid, reduce or defer. "Reasonable" pension deductions refer to voluntary contributions to a pension plan in which an employee has the option of participating. Common voluntary plans include 401K plans and matched retirement savings plans. When examining pension deductions to determine what is reasonable, one must analyze the entire pension package that is available, both voluntary and involuntary, and the chosen level of participation. As a practical matter, participation in a qualified but voluntary pension plan with some matching funds provided by the employer will likely be allowed because such plans are so very cost-effective for the payor.

Deduction number eight was recently added. Previously, the court had no direction on how to allocate support to multiple families. Now the court subtracts any child support that is currently being paid by prior order when a payor is supporting children in more than one family. The amendment makes it easy to apply the guidelines and to define net income. Prior maintenance awards are not deducted from the obligor's gross income to determine the net.

It is important to note that children born of subsequent relationships are allocated less support. For example, if a payor earns $2,000 net monthly income and has a prior child support obligation of $500 from a first marriage, then net income for determining support for a child from a subsequent marriage will be only $1,500 and the award will be $375, or $125 less than the first child.

The statute states that the guidelines need not be followed in every case, but requires that courts which deviate from the guidelines make express findings of fact showing the reasons for the upward or downward departure. That statute further states that the court should consider a variety of factors, including the guidelines, to set or modify child support. These factors include:

1. All earnings, income and resources of the parents, including real and personal property.
2. The financial needs and resources, the physical and emotional condition, and educational needs of the child.
3. The standard of living that the child would have enjoyed if the marriage had not been dissolved.
4. Any government entitlement or welfare benefits paid for or on behalf of the child.
5. Other debts that the parents may have incurred.

Minnesota Statutes Section 518.55, subd. 5(b) (1-5) (1988).

Debts to private creditors are limited in relevancy, and debts are not considered if the right of support has been assigned to a public welfare agency. If the child receives public assistance, the payor makes child support payments to the agency as partial reimbursement for that aid. However, in non-welfare situations, limited debts can be considered. Only debts incurred for the reasonable support of the child or the parent, or debts necessary to generate income, may be considered.

If a party asks the court to consider debts to support a deviation from the guidelines, that party must provide careful documentation of those debts: current bill statements, what goods or services were purchased, the outstanding balance and the monthly payment. Regardless of how long it will take to pay off those debts, an 18-month grace period for the reduction of child support is the maximum allowed by law.

If the custodial parent is debt-ridden due to living costs of the child or himself, or due to expenses incurred in generating income, payments may be increased to help cover that debt. When child support is ordered, special protective statutes allow for streamlined collection of child support. If child support is increased because of the custodial parent's debt, and the payor is ordered to contribute to this debt through increased child support, the payment shall still be considered child support and subject to wage-withholding and other remedies available to a payee entitled to child support, even though part of this payment is actually intended for joint debts.

Although the court may consider factors for variation, these guidelines are imposed rather rigidly in an effort to be fair and uniform in the establishment of child support levels. With the thousands of fact-specific cases before them every year and a limited time to examine each case, most judges and referees find that uniform imposition of the child support guidelines is the fairest way to deal with all of them.

If you have a decree that was entered before the child support guidelines were established, the guidelines will be applied to a modification even though not in effect at the time of the original hearing. In many cases, the application of the guidelines to child support orders that were originally entered before 1983 substantially increases the payor's obligation. However, the guidelines alone will not operate to increase support. In order to increase support, one must first show a substantial change of circumstances as defined by the statute. The issue of modification of support levels is discussed in the next chapter.

There are some practical aspects to consider when applying the guidelines. At present, the statute states that net income may not include the income of the payor's spouse.

For example, assume when John and Jane divorce, John earns $2,000 net per month; Jane is awarded physical custody of their two children, and John pays Jane $600 per month support. Further, assume that John marries Ann two years later, and Ann's income is also $2,000 per month. John and Ann now have $4,000 per month, less child support of $600, which is only 15% of the new couple's income.

It is obviously unfair to charge Ann for John's children from his marriage to Jane, but one might be tempted to argue that his standard of living has escalated. If his mortgage and utility payments are now shared, those expenses are halved. However, at present there is no provision in Minnesota law to support the argument. However, the court will consider any other income to the household when determining the household expenses. Contributions of a spouse or a roommate to those expenses will be factored into the determination.

The child support guidelines do not specifically consider the income of the custodial parent. At lower income levels, the guidelines-determined child support can be a substantial burden to the payor. For example, if a payor earns $900 per month, he pays $243 per month for two children. This leaves only $657 per month for his own living expenses. The custodial parent may have an income two or three times that of the payor, and the statute does say that all earnings, income and resources of *both* parents should be considered. But the statute provides no guidance for determining whether a deviation should be made or by how much.

Our state laws often develop from models in other states. In Iowa, the child support guidelines specifically consider the recipient's income. However, no such law now exists in Minnesota.

Special problems also arise when the decree orders shared physical custody of children. Many parties choose to have their children live part of the year with each parent. However, if each parent is housing and feeding the children for a substantial portion of the year, the financial duty of each party to the other cannot easily be defined by the guidelines.

Minnesota courts have approved a "cross-support" formula, which applies the guidelines to each spouse's income and adjusts the amount each party pays by determining the portion of the year the children reside with each parent.

For our example:

1. There are two children.
2. The children spend summers with Jane (3 full months), and the school year with John.
3. John earns $2,500 net per month, and Jane has a net monthly income of $1,800.

If John owed Jane support for every month, John would pay 30%, or $750 per month. If Jane owed John support for each month, Jane would pay $600.

In our example, John should receive support for nine months and pay for three. However, as a practical matter, both John and Jane support households all year which allow the children to live with each of them part of the year.

John's total support obligation is $750 for three months, or $2,250. Jane's total support obligation is $600 for nine months, or $5,400. The difference is $3,150.

Jane could be ordered to pay John $262.50 per month (1/12th of the difference). However, the court does not require use of this formula. A trial court may apply any formula which fairly reflects the law and the financial needs and resources of each party.

For example, during the school year John may have no daycare costs for the children, while Jane may have to pay for full-time care during the summer. Also, if John and Jane no longer reside near one another, there may be significant transportation costs.

Each unique fact situation must either be carefully negotiated or presented to the court in detail, because the law does not mandate specific solutions.

CHAPTER 8

If I think my order to receive (or pay) support is unreasonable, how do I change it?

Prior to July 1, 1987, a person who fell behind on support payments could ask the court to have unmade payments forgiven because of past inability to pay. This request usually was made in response to a motion for collection of unpaid support. However, since July 1, 1987, a person ordered to pay support is obligated to petition the court to amend the support order if the person is unable to pay. Unmade payments that come due before the payor starts the process of requesting an adjustment can no longer be forgiven.

The court does not recognize as valid some reasons for inability to pay. For example, if your income is seasonal, it is your obligation to budget so that payments are made year-round, or to pay more in months when income is higher, thereby prepaying the support for lower-income months. Monthly support should be established using the annual income figure of a seasonal worker, not on the high-earning months alone. Unemployment compensation is generally included in annual income.

Most support orders entered since 1984 have a formula for a biennial (every two years) cost-of-living adjustment. The formula is based on inflation and the general economy, not on the parties' needs or income. Those cost-of-living adjustments are addressed in Chapter 10. However, cost-of-living increases do not always reflect the needs of children or the resources of divorced parents as they change over time.

When first seeking a change, always consider the possibility of negotiating a new agreement. If two people can agree to change the amount of support, the modified agreement will generally be approved by a court. If this is not possible, you will need to ask the court for an adjustment.

The law tries to protect both those who pay and those who receive support from having unreasonable orders imposed upon them. However, because the law tries to balance competing interests, and not every fact situation is clearly addressed by the law, modifying support can be complicated. To initiate a change, have your current order reviewed by an attorney to determine how the original support amount was calculated.

Next, have your lawyer review your current budget and expenses. If you have specific, separate, child-related expenses that have changed over time, be sure to explain these changes. For example, a toddler's needs may be modest—clothes, diapers and food—compared to a teenager's needs: extracurricular school expenses, car insurance and haircuts. A particularized budget of all parties' needs is essential.

Finally, you need to know what the other party earned at the time of the divorce (or the last support order) compared to present earnings. This information can be obtained through discovery, the formal process of information-sharing between attorneys. A lawyer can submit lists of questions or requests for documents, or conduct live question-and-answer sessions called "depositions." The cost of each process varies, and your lawyer can best choose the methods that are right for your case.

The lawyer petitions the court by making a motion and begins gathering the facts. The parties and their attorneys then appear before the judge to highlight the most important points, which is done in a brief statement made by the attorney. Although a motion hearing may be short, the majority of the work has occurred before the court appearance. Your attorney will develop legal arguments and prepare evidence to be filed with the court. The judge may make a decision immediately or may take the case "under advisement," which means the court will review the case and issue a written decision.

In order to modify a child support order, the party requesting the modification must prove that there has been a substantial change of circumstances making the old order unfair in light of the current facts. This involves a two-step analysis. First, it requires a showing that one or more of the following circumstances exist:

1. increased or decreased earnings of either party;
2. increased or decreased needs of either party; and
3. the receipt of welfare benefits.

Minnesota Statutes Section 518.64, subd. 2 (1988).

Applying the third category is simple. If a party did not receive public assistance benefits at the time of the last order, but does now, that fact can be easily proved.

Proving increased or decreased income or expenses is more complex. First, the change must be "substantial." There is no legal definition of this term, but a change of 10% is probably not sufficient to modify an order. The facts of each case determine what is "substantial."

If a court decides that a substantial change of circumstances has occurred, it must take the second step of the analysis. It must find that the changed circumstances are so significant as to make the original order unfair and unreasonable. To be fair, the court must consider the factors used to determine the current amount of support and the resources and needs of the parents and the children.

The court will examine what caused the change. For example, to consider a decrease in overtime pay which formerly contributed heavily to a party's income, clear proof is necessary.

If a change of jobs has decreased a party's income, a payor will be expected to give a rational explanation for the job change. Obviously, courts are sympathetic to job changes that are outside the payor's control. If the payor's job is eliminated or if the payor's employer has gone out of business, that party must document the situation.

If a payor's job changes and the resulting income decrease is voluntary, the court may consider not only the current income, but also the payor's *capacity* to earn income. If a payor gets a promotion and a higher salary, it may be reasonable to increase support; however, if the new job requires relocation, the cost of living in another city may offset the raise, and modification may not occur.

The law limits the changes in income or expense that may form the basis for a modification. Excluded changes are:

1. the giving of gifts;
2. remarriage;
3. additional children; or
4. the income of a new spouse.

The legislature has set these limits to help judges make equitable decisions; nonetheless, some inequities exist. A new spouse may double a household's income, but this is irrelevant. A new baby will clearly increase expenses, but this is rarely considered in modifying support.

If you are ordered to pay support and you do not believe you have the financial resources to pay it, you must take the initiative to have your order changed; modification is your responsibility. You may not simply reduce your payments because your income has decreased or your expenses increased. If you fall behind in your payments, the court may recognize that your income has substantially decreased, but may not, by law, be able to forgive arrearages that have accrued. The party moving for either a reduction or an increase has the burden of proof. This means that he or she must provide sufficient proof of present circumstances as well as changed circumstances.

If a court finds that a substantial change of circumstances has occurred, and the change makes the original decree unfair and unreasonable, it must then determine the amount of increase or decrease. To do this, it must consider:

a. the financial resources and needs of a child;
b. the financial resources and needs of the custodial parent;
c. the standard of living the child would have enjoyed had the marriage not been dissolved;
d. the physical and emotional condition of the child, and his educational needs; and

e. the financial resources and needs of the non-custodial parent.

Minnesota Statutes Section 518.17, subd. 4 (1988).

Child support is different from spousal maintenance. Please look to another section in this book for a discussion of changes in spousal maintenance.

Our state legislature meets every year, and for the past several years has made a variety of changes related to support, maintenance and modifications. If the law and facts of your case do not present the result you want today, you should consult your lawyer about how the law may change in the future and how these changes could affect your case.

In general, you should consider seeking legal advice on support modification if:

1. your last order is five years old or more; or
2. you know or suspect that one or both parties' incomes have changed more than 10%; or
3. specific expenses, particularly those related to a child or a party with special needs, have markedly increased or decreased.

These facts should be evaluated in light of the number of years remaining in your support obligation.

CHAPTER 9

What can I do to receive my child support payments on time each month?

Non-payment of judicially ordered child support has become a national problem of serious magnitude. A 1984 census estimated that more than 40% of families entitled to receive support do not actually receive it. In response to this growing non-payment epidemic, Minnesota Statutes attempt to address the problems by providing collection methods.

Minnesota Statutes Section 518.611 provides that if a payor falls 30 days behind in child support or spousal maintenance, the person entitled to receive the support can have those payments directly withheld from the payor's payroll check. However, this does not happen automatically; the person entitled to the support must take special steps.

First, one must send a letter to the payor. This "warning" letter must include several specific statements:

1. The payee has determined that the payor is 30 days in arrears in payment.
2. The payor must become current in 15 days or, in the alternative, make a proper motion to the court within 15 days addressing the issue of late payments.
3. If one of these options is not completed in 15 days, wage-withholding will be instituted.

The letter must state the exact amount of support that is due, but has not been paid, along with any other payments that are due, or will become due in 15 days.

Keep a copy of the letter and proof that you mailed it. Either send it by registered or certified mail, or have a notarized statement signed by the person who actually mailed the letter.

If you receive no response within 15 days (plus three for mailing), send these documents to the employer:

1. a letter explaining the request to have support withheld from wages;
2. a copy of the warning letter; and
3. a copy of your court order.

The court order is usually contained in your judgment and decree, or it may be included in a subsequent order modifying support. Often the statutory language which details the wage-withholding order and the procedure is contained in a preprinted attachment entitled "Appendix A." Be certain that the copy you send the employer has this attachment confirming your right to income withholding.

Keep copies of all of these documents. You should start receiving support regularly, directly from the employer. If within two weeks you do not, call the payroll department and inquire about their policy for wage-withholding. An employer who ignores a properly documented request for wage-withholding may be liable for amounts that are not properly paid to you.

As of October 1, 1987, in Hennepin County and in some rural counties, every new or reviewed order for child support or spousal maintenance will be subject to mandatory, immediate wage-withholding. This eliminates the 30-day arrearages wait. This pilot project will determine whether automatic wage-withholding is cost-effective by increasing the number of claimants who actually receive their support.

It takes two to six weeks to establish the withholding process before the first check is received. However, once administrative details are correctly in place, a recipient should receive support on a routine basis, in the total amount ordered. If you are subject to automatic wage-withholding, both payors and recipients should keep a log of payments made or received. Errors can occur, and it is your responsibility, not the county's, to document them.

Automatic wage-withholding does not solve the collection problem for all families. Self-employed individuals present a particular problem because there is no third-party employer to implement the process. The self-employed individual is instructed by the county administering automatic wage-withholding to send payment to the county, which forwards it to the recipient. If the individual fails to do this, there is no simple administrative procedure for recovering payments, and a motion must be brought before the court.

There is also a significant collection problem with people who are seasonally employed, or who receive irregular compensation, such as commissioned salespeople. The law attempts to calculate support on an annual basis, and a payor is instructed to establish a payment budget. However, the law does not give a simple formula for these situations, and consequently they pose special problems.

Finally, some support recipients find that payments rarely, if ever, fall 30 days in arrears, but are often paid unpredictably, in part rather than in full, or are routinely less than 30 days late. If there is an established pattern, document it. The court may find that wage-withholding is justified in this situation.

The automatic income withholding project will end July 31, 1989, unless the legislature acts before that date to make it a statewide program. Therefore, this area of the law is far from settled at the time this book goes to print.

Traditional enforcement for unpaid support is a "contempt of court" proceeding. There are two classifications of contempt powers—civil and criminal—and each has a different purpose. Criminal contempt is used to punish, and civil contempt is used to obtain compliance. Family courts most frequently use civil contempt.

The requirements for the proper exercise of civil contempt are:

a. a court must have subject matter jurisdiction;
b. there must be a clear definition of the acts to be performed;
c. there must be notice of the acts to be performed and the time within which to comply;

d. the party seeking to enforce the acts must apply for enforcement and give specific grounds for complaint;
e. a hearing must be held after due notice at which the non-performing party can show compliance or provide an explanation for failing to comply;
f. there must be a formal determination by the court of a failure to comply;
g. there must be an opportunity for the non-performing party to show an inability to perform and that a good faith effort was made; and
h. there must be an ability to gain release through compliance or a good-faith effort to comply.

While contempt is usually sought when a payor fails to make payments, it can also be used when an obligor fails to obtain medical or life insurance ordered by the court.

CHAPTER 10

Am I eligible to receive a cost-of-living adjustment in the child support I receive?

Since 1983, each final decree of dissolution which contains an order for child support also includes a provision for a cost-of-living adjustment.

This clause allows for an adjustment to be made every two years to account for general increases in inflation, or the cost of living. This cost-of-living adjustment (COLA) does not depend on increases in the payor's income or increased needs of the child. In fact, it is effective even if the resources of the recipient have increased. It operates merely to adjust the original award into today's dollars.

COLAs are often overlooked. If your decree includes this language, it may be in small print in an attachment known as "Appendix A," along with many other statutory rights and notices.

To take advantage of a COLA, the payee must make several calculations based on the consumer price index, and give notice to the payor of the effective date and amount of the COLA increase.

It is well worth the effort, because if inflation is 10% over a period of two years, and if your child support order is $500 per month, then the adjustment is worth a total of $1,200 for a two-year period. The steps to implement this procedure may seem complex when read as a whole, but when broken down to a checklist they can easily be done without additional advice from your attorney.

All COLA increases go into effect on May 1 of the year you give notice of your intent to claim the increase. First, you need to know *when* to apply for the adjustment.

If your divorce decree was issued before May 1 of the year in which it was granted, you may apply for the COLA in two years. For example, if you were divorced in February, 1986, the first COLA would be effective May 1, 1988. If your decree was entered after May 1, you will need to wait until the following spring. If you were divorced November 1, 1986, the first COLA would be available May 1, 1989, two years and six months later. If you attempted to implement it in May, 1988, only 18 months would have passed and the law requires that at least 24 months pass before implementing an increase as of May 1.

Once you have implemented one COLA, you may apply again at two-year intervals. If your COLA went into effect in an odd-numbered year, you can reapply in the next odd-numbered year. If your child support is increased or decreased by court order, this whole schedule starts again, because the date of your original decree is replaced by the date of the new order.

Once you have determined which May 1 is the date to implement your COLA, follow these simple steps:

1. *On March 15:* Call the public library to determine the change in the cost of living index between the date of your last order or adjustment and today's date. Ask for the "Consumer Price Index for all Urban Consumers" or the "Consumer Price Index for Wage Earners and Clerical, Minneapolis–St. Paul." Apply this formula to your support award (an example is provided).
2. *No Later Than April 7:* Write a letter to the payor stating you intend to claim a COLA increase, and state the amount of the increase to be effective May 1 (a form letter is included later in this chapter).

The payor has a right to object to implementation of the COLA. However, to make that objection effective, he or she must make a motion to the family court, and must serve upon you notice of that motion between the date of the letter's receipt and May 1 of that year. You may give notice any time between January 1 and April 7, but this suggested timetable gives you the most up-to-date inflation figures and tactically limits the time for objection.

The letter must be mailed no later than April 7, because the payor is entitled to 20 days notice and you must add three days for mailing time.

If the payor objects, the court may waive the COLA only if:

1. the payor's occupation or income provides for no cost-of-living adjustment; or
2. your decree, or most recent order, provides for other periodic adjustments.

These are the only two appropriate reasons for waiver of a COLA. If the payor does not ask for a reduction of total support but simply objects to the COLA, you or your attorney must appear at a hearing. The burden is on the party objecting to the increase to show that he or she is entitled to one of the exceptions.

The Consumer Price Index for Urban Consumers (CPI-U) was formerly computed every other month. As of January, 1987,it is computed only semi-annually, for June 30 to December 31. Choose the date closest in time to the order in your case.

The CPI-U is a statistic compiled by the government to compare inflation figures for various years. The calculation began by assigning arbitrarily to the year 1960 the number 100, representing $1. In the 1980s, with the CPI-U at more than $300, $1 in 1960 would have bought what $3 buys today.

Here is an example of application of the COLA formula. John and Jane were divorced in February, 1986. Therefore, the first COLA increase will be available on May 1, 1988. The CPI-U for February, 1986, was 336.2, and for December 31, 1987, it was 355.7 in the Minneapolis/St. Paul area.

The COLA formula looks like this:

1. Subtract the earlier number from the December 31, 1987, number:
   355.7 − 336.2 = 19.5
2. Divide 19.5 by the earlier number:
   $\frac{19.5}{336.2}$ = .0580
3. Multiply .0580 by 100.
   .0580 x 100 = 5.80%

Jane originally received $500 per month from John. Application of the COLA will increase payments by 5.80%, or $29, per month. The new monthly payments will be $529, and over two years the increase amounts to $696.

In 1990, when Jane goes through the process again, she will apply the inflation figure to $529 per month, not the original $500, and will rely on inflation figures for 1988 and 1990.

If you have missed prior dates where you could have claimed a COLA (for example, if it has been four years since your divorce), you can use the formula from the date of your decree to May 1 of next year, and you can compute each two-year period separately.

In our example, if Jane did not apply in 1988, in 1990 she could first compute the increase between 1986 and 1988, and then the increase between 1988 and 1990 could be applied to the "new" 1988 figure.

If inflation was 3% from 1986 to 1988, and 6% from 1988 to 1990, then the increase effective May 1, 1990, would be:

Original Order	$500
+ 3% (1986-88)	15
1987 Total	$515
+ 6% (1988-90)	31
1990 Total	$546

Unfortunately, cost-of-living increases do not apply to decrees entered before August 1, 1983. However, if your decree was modified after August 1, 1983, the court may have added in the COLA. Check the language in your modified order.

As of 1988, a cost-of-living increase is also applied to maintenance awards, unless the parties agree in writing to waive the COLA.

The following form letter can serve as notice of your intent to claim the COLA. Just fill in the blanks:

COST-OF-LIVING ADJUSTMENT

Dear (Payor),

I write to give you notice of my intent to implement my cost-of-living adjustment on child support.

I have calculated the increase in the cost of living between ___/___/___ (the date of your divorce or the date of your last order), and 12/31/___ to be ___%.

Your child support obligation is currently $___, and shall increase by ___%, or $___, to a new figure of $__________ on May 1, 19___.

Please commence paying the higher amount on that date. If you are on wage-withholding, please inform your employer of this adjustment.

Very truly yours,

________(Payee)________

If your spouse is paying support to a county as collection agent, and/or has wage-withholding, send a copy of this letter to the employer and your payment counselor.

Keep copies of all the letters and worksheets you used to calculate the increase. Note the date you mailed the letter. You may send it by registered mail, but you are not required to do so.

This worksheet may be helpful in calculating your increase.

Date of order or decree: ________________

CPI-U for ______(date)______ : ______(X)______

(closest in time to order available)

CPI-U for 12/31 last year: ______(Y)______

$$\frac{X - Y}{Y} \times 100 = \text{increase}$$

Amount of Support $________

___% of Amount $________

New Support $________

CHAPTER 11

What are the tax consequences of a dissolution?

Maintenance, or alimony, is deductible by the payor and taxable to the payee. In 1988, at the federal tax rate of 28%, a monthly maintenance payment of $1,500 actually cost the payor $1,005. The recipient of that $1,500 payment received $1,005 after taxes at the 28% rate.

Child support, on the other hand, is neither taxable nor deductible. You should know what your marginal tax brackets are. This information may be critical to negotiating a stipulation.

Personal exemptions have increased from $1,080 in 1986 to $2,000 in 1989. Therefore, the ability to claim your children as exemptions has become more valuable. If you can declare even one child, you will be entitled to file a "head-of-household" return. Taxpayers filing as heads of household pay a lower tax rate than single taxpayers.

If you are the party responsible for paying maintenance or child support, you may wish to consider investing a portion of any of the gains from the sale of marital property into a tax-exempt or interest-bearing account to help defray your future payment obligations.

Both parties would benefit by incorporating into their stipulation a cost-of-living adjustment on both maintenance and child support payments (discussed in detail elsewhere in this book). This provision saves both parties the cost of returning to court for such increases and takes into account the effects of annual inflation.

Other tax considerations of which you should be aware involve the sale or transfer of property. It is usually more advantageous to transfer property than to sell it. If you are considering selling your house or securities, you may be subject to an increased tax liability on the proceeds. However, property transferred with an appreciated value (such as a house or securities) in exchange for relinquishment of marital rights to a pension plan or other property is not taxable as gain to the transferror.

In contrast, property settlement payments may have tax consequences. If you sell the house and pay a portion of the proceeds to your spouse, that property settlement will not be deductible.

If your financial situation is complex, be sure a tax attorney or an accountant examines any stipulation that you consider. He or she can give you invaluable advice not only about maintenance and child support issues but about the sale and transfer of property as well.

A portion of your legal and accounting fees will be deductible. Fees for any work which was done to help you obtain income or for advice regarding maintenance, income property, securities and taxes are deductible. Request an itemized billing to help you identify the items that qualify for a tax deduction.

CHAPTER 12

Who will provide for our family's health insurance?

The wage-earner in a family is the insurance provider. As of 1987, *Minnesota Statutes Section 62A.2* provides:

> A policy of health and accident insurance coverage cannot terminate for a spouse solely as a result of a break-up in a marital relationship.

This means that your health coverage cannot be discontinued by the insurance company only because of divorce, but must continue until:

a. the former spouse becomes covered under any other plan; or
b. the date coverage would terminate under the policy.

A former spouse is also given the option of converting the health coverage to his/her own policy without showing proof of insurability. The cost of such coverage, and who will for pay it, are separate considerations.

In the case of dependent children, the court will order the person paying child support to name the minor child as beneficiary on any health and dental insurance available through the employer, and if the spouse's coverage is available at no additional cost, then the insured must provide it.

If there are no minor children, the insured is not obligated to *pay* for a former spouse's coverage. The cost of such coverage is a negotiable item to be considered when you draft your stipulation.

CHAPTER 13

Should I change my name?

A much-loved child has many names, but society's official name for a person must follow specific rules. Constantly changing societal values are reflected in the new name designs selected by married couples. Women, though not required to do so, traditionally changed their surname to their husband's upon marriage. By custom, then, children took their father's name. Today, a man may take his wife's name, one or both may use hyphenated names, or each might use a separate last name. The only legal limitation is that a surname may not be selected for fraudulent purposes.

Divorcing women, to satisfy both emotional and legal needs, may wish to resume using their maiden names. This can happen by operation of the judgment and decree.

Whether you change your name is a matter of personal preference. If you do change your name, other actions should quickly follow:

1. notify all creditors promptly;
2. correct your driver's license within 30 days;
3. notify the Social Security Administration; and
4. be sure that a notice of the change is attached to all existing legal records.

When changing your name, set forth your new name exactly as you wish it to be in the judgment and decree. This includes your full middle name. If you list only the middle initial, your middle initial becomes your middle name for purposes of all future legal documents.

When deciding whether to change your name, you may want to consider the fact that your name will be different from your children's. Courts are extremely reluctant to allow children's names to be changed. A divorced parent may not change a child's name without the other parent's consent or without clear and compelling evidence that the substantial welfare of the child necessitates such a change. The court also frowns upon informal change of a child's name, because a child's name is most likely established through everyday usage.

The courts have said that neither parent has a superior right initially to decide the child's surname. However, once either the mother or the father's name, or a combination, has been given to a child, any change must promote the child's best interests.

These criteria will be considered in determining the child's best interests:

1. the child's preference;
2. the effect of the change of the child's surname on the preservation and development of the child's relationship with each parent;
3. the length of time the child has borne a given name;
4. the degree of community respect associated with the present and proposed name; and
5. the difficulties, harassment or embarrassment that the child may experience from bearing the present or the proposed surname.

If two people bear a child out of wedlock, their subsequent marriage does not automatically convert the child's name to the father's. Parents may presume that this occurs, but it does not. The child will retain the surname appearing on its birth certificate. An application for a name change is necessary if the parents wish the child to have a last name different from that appearing on the birth certificate.

There are limits on the kind of name a person may choose. In a Minnesota case, a man wished to change his name to the number "1069." The trial court refused the change on the grounds that designating a person by a number was an "abject dehumanization and totalitarian deprivation of dignified human privacy." The Supreme Court agreed.

CHAPTER 14

When is my divorce finally over?

Divorce ends only the marriage, not the relationship. The entry of the final decree does not really terminate your relationship with your spouse, especially if maintenance or child support payments continue. After the dissolution, you may return to court on any number of post-dissolution issues. Therefore, the character of your relationship is simply altered after a divorce.

Love and friendship are not requirements to clear, simple communication. A divorced couple who can still communicate with one another have the potential to solve the inevitable problems which will occur. They will save themselves much time, emotional energy and money. Where children are involved, their welfare and your peace of mind will be intertwined with your problem-solving abilities. For these reasons, you will need to maintain an operational relationship with your ex-spouse.

The psychological end to a divorce can be achieved only when the acrimony and bitterness have ceased. Not everyone experiences this final stage, but keeping the lines of communication open can make adjustment easier and speed the emotional healing process.

CHAPTER 15

Can an antenuptial agreement protect me if I remarry?

Dewy-eyed romantics marrying for the first time may consider antenuptial agreements to be abhorrent, poison pills empowered with a self-fulfilling prophecy. They will claim, "If you expect a marriage to fail, it will." The "older, but wiser" person entering into a second marriage is more cautious and will value the antenuptial agreement as a safeguard.

The primary objective of an antenuptial agreement is to take any surprise out of the end of a marriage. Such an agreement defines property rights, duties and expectations of the parties. If used correctly, it can eliminate false expectations.

Historically, antenuptial agreements were limited to inheritance issues. They began as tools used to settle property rights when one of the parties died. Typically, they were used if a party entered a second marriage and substantial property was involved. In other words, they were the domain of the rich. Public opinion of antenuptial agreements has not always been positive, because dividing property in advance seems to anticipate the breakdown of a marriage. Antenuptial agreements which distribute property in the event of a divorce have been upheld only during the last two decades.

The modern view favors use of these agreements because, if properly drafted, they are preventive measures that may keep potential litigants out of court. They can be useful estate planning tools, and there are many reasons why such preplanning is valuable. Antenuptial agreements can establish property rights, simplify finances to prevent inadvertent commingling of funds, avoid confusion about the economic aspects of a relationship, and generally provide a sense of security for the two parties involved. A valid antenuptial agreement must be enforceable, and to be enforceable it should contain these elements:

1. it must be in writing;
2. it must be signed voluntarily;
3. there must be no duress, misrepresentation or coercion in obtaining the agreement;
4. it must be a conscionable agreement;
5. there must be full disclosure of the amount, description and value of both parties' property;
6. there should be an adequate lapse of time between the signing of the agreement and the wedding day;
7. both parties must fully understand the issues in the agreement;
8. the parties should have separate counsel to accomplish the agreement; and
9. the parties should avoid unenforceable issues.

As you can see from this long list of requirements, there is a chance that your antenuptial agreement will not be enforceable. It can be attacked if any one of these elements is missing. Even the simplest and most obvious is critical. In Minnesota, an oral antenuptial agreement was held to be invalid. It must be written and signed.

When a court is asked to consider if an agreement is fair and reasonable, it examines a variety of factors, including:

a. age of the parties when the contract is made;
b. behavior of the parties after the marriage, indicating understanding of the antenuptial agreement;
c. property owned by each party; and
d. potential income of each party.

An honest disclosure of each party's property is listed as one requirement, and you should be sure your agreement lists all of the property owned by *both* parties. In a 1982 case, our Supreme Court stated that a general and approximate knowledge of net worth was sufficient disclosure.

Adequate time is needed between the signing of the agreement and the wedding date. In Minnesota, an antenuptial agreement signed five days before the wedding was held to be invalid. If an agreement is signed a short time before the actual wedding, a party might argue that there was not enough time to read and understand the document, or that the document was the product of coercion.

Certain things should not logically be included in an antenuptial agreement, and others should legally not be included. Legally, the right to receive maintenance cannot be contracted away far into the future. The same is true of potential child support payments for future children. It is also important to note that property later purchased and owned in joint tenancy cannot be considered part of the property included in an antenuptial agreement because it is marital property.

Logically, things that should not be included can be characterized as non-enforceable, far-reaching, and non-economic issues. These issues are often lifestyle issues, yet some people insist on trying to stipulate such unenforceable matters.

A young couple in Missouri insisted on including some ridiculous elements in their antenuptial agreement: agreeing never to go to bed angry and designating who would vacuum the rugs and who would wash the dishes. Sexual expectations were outlined as well and, predictably, the marriage dissolved nine months later.

Issues like these have no place in antenuptial agreements any more than questions relating to the care, custody, support and education of future children. In what religion children will be raised, where couples will vacation, and who will do which household chores are all inappropriate items for such a document.

Careful preplanning and caution are the bywords which should guide the construction of your antenuptial agreement. Be sure to consider the tax ramifications of property transfers created by the agreement.

An important case, *McGee v. Johnson,* is before the Supreme Court as this book is being written. It addresses the enforceability of various provisions in an antenuptial agreement. This is an unsettled area of the law at present, and you should check with your attorney before drafting an antenuptial agreement.

CHAPTER 16

When should I see an attorney and what should I take with me?

If you are experiencing marital problems, it is wise first to seek marriage counseling from a licensed psychologist or professional counselor. If your marriage can be saved, that option should be thoroughly explored. Even if your spouse refuses to be involved and you attend counseling alone, a counselor can be invaluable to you in clarifying your alternatives and serving as an impartial sounding board for your ideas.

If you decide to consult an attorney, you need not be ready to proceed immediately with a divorce. An initial consultation is usually free; however, check on this with the individual attorney. In order to help you be effectively prepared and use an initial consultation to the greatest benefit, we are providing a client information questionnaire. If you prepare this financial and personal profile ahead of time, any attorney will be better equipped to advise you on the specifics of your case, rather than speaking in broad generalities. You, in turn, will be better able to assess your situation, decide if you want to proceed, and determine if that lawyer is right for you.

This preparation can also save you money. Most attorneys have hourly rates, and the more work you do yourself, the lower your bill will be.

Be candid with your attorney; remember that an attorney/client relationship is a privileged one, and anything you disclose is confidential.

CHESTNUT & BROOKS, P.A.
Client Information Questionnaire
Marriage Dissolution

So that we will be able to answer your questions and handle your case in a prompt and efficient manner, it is important that you attempt to answer the following questions fully and accurately. If you need additional space for an answer, you may use the back of a page. The completed questionnaire will be kept confidential and will remain in our possession.

Date: ________________ Referred By: ______________________

Personal Information–Client

1. Full Name ______________________________________
2. Present Street Address ____________________________
   City/State __________ County ______________ Zip ________
3. Home Phone ____________ Business Phone ____________
4. Social Security Number ___________________________
5. Length of Residence in Minnesota __________________
6. Birthplace ____________ Birth Date __________ Age ______
7. Religion _______________________________________
8. Highest Level of Education ______ Year Completed ______
9. Present Health ___________________________________
10. Physician or Clinic _______________________________
11. Are you presently in the military service of the United States? ____
12. Name and telephone number of person (other than your spouse) who would be most likely always to know where you can be reached _________________________________
    Relationship to you _________________________________

Personal Information–Spouse

1. Full Name ______________________________________
2. Present Street Address ____________________________
   City/State __________ County ______________ Zip ________

3. Home Phone ____________ Business Phone ____________
4. Social Security Number ____________
5. Length of Residence in Minnesota ____________
6. Birthplace ____________ Birth Date ____________ Age ______
7. Religion ____________
8. Highest Level of Education ______ Year Completed ______
9. Present Health ____________
10. Physician or Clinic ____________
11. Is your spouse presently in the Military Service of the United States? ____________

Employment Information–Client

1. Employer ____________
2. Address ____________
3. Occupation ____________
4. Length of Time with this Employer ____________
5. Gross Earnings ____________ Per ____________
6. Net Earnings ____________ Per ____________
7. How many exemptions do you claim? ____________
8. Itemize those items that are deducted from your paycheck:

   Federal ____________ State ____________

   FICA ____________ Medical/Dental ____________

   Other (Specify) ____________
9. Any other income (overtime, bonuses, commissions, other employment)? ____________
10. Do you have a pension plan with this or any previous employer? ____________
11. Any profit sharing? ____________
12. Detail your prior work experience ____________

    ____

    ____

    ____

Employment Information–Spouse

1. Employer ______________________
2. Address ______________________
3. Occupation ______________________
4. Length of Time with this Employer ______________
5. Gross Earnings ______________ Per ______________
6. Net Earnings ______________ Per ______________
7. How many exemptions does your spouse claim? ________
8. Itemize those items that are deducted from your spouse's paycheck:

   Federal ______________ State ______________

   FICA ______________ Medical/Dental ______________

   Other (Specify) ______________________
9. Any other income (overtime, bonuses, commissions, other employment)? ______________________
10. Does your spouse have a pension plan with this or any previous employer? ______________________
11. Any profit sharing? ______________________
12. Detail your spouse's prior work experience ______________

    ____

    ____

    ____

Marital Information

1. Date of present marriage ______________________
2. City, county and state where you were married ______________

   ____
3. Describe any action that has been taken by either you or your spouse to dissolve this marriage ______________

   ____
4. State the date, purpose and individuals involved in any counseling of you and/or your spouse ______________

   ____

   ____

5. Do you feel there is any chance to save this marriage? ___
6. Summarize your spouse's conduct that you feel is causing you to seek a dissolution of your marriage ___________

____

____

____

7. What would be your spouse's primary complaints about you? ___________

____

8. Are you and your spouse living together? ___________
9. If not, the date of separation ___________

   Note: Minnesota law requires that a Petition for Dissolution address the question of the possible pregnancy of a Petitioner or Respondent.

10. Are you, or is your spouse, pregnant? ___________
11. Date of last sexual relations with spouse ___________

Other Marital Information–Client

1. Were you previously married? ___________
2. When were you divorced? ___________
3. City, county and state of divorce ___________
4. Names and ages of minor children by previous marriage:

____

____

____

5. Who received custody? ___________
6. Are you receiving or paying maintenance from a previous marriage? _______ How much? ___________ per _______
7. Are you receiving or paying child support from a previous marriage? _______ How much? ___________ per _______
8. Assets received ___________

Other Marital Information–Spouse

1. Was your spouse previously married? ___________
2. When was your spouse divorced? ___________

3. City, county and state of divorce ______________________
4. Names and ages of minor children by spouse's previous marriage: ______________________
____
5. Who received custody? ______________________
6. Is your spouse receiving or paying maintenance from a previous marriage? ______ How much? ______ per______
7. Is your spouse receiving or paying child support from a previous marriage? ______ How much? ______ per______
8. Assets received ______________________

Children from this Marriage or Adopted into this Marriage

1. Children's names, ages and birth dates:
2. Do the children now live with Client ______ Spouse ______ Both ______
3. Do you want custody of these children? ______________
4. Do you expect a contest over who should have custody of the children? ______ Why? ______________________
____
____

Assets

A. *Homestead*

1. Address ______________________
2. City ______________________ State ____________
3. Do you have a copy of the deed to this Property? ______
4. When was this homestead purchased? ______ Cost? ______
5. Amount of downpayment ______________________
6. Source of downpayment ______________________
7. In whose name(s) is the title? ______________________
8. What is the present value? ______________________
9. Present mortgage or contract for deed balance ______
10. Monthly payment ______________________
11. To whom are the payments made? ______________

12. Does the payment include taxes?__________
    insurance?__________
13. What are the yearly taxes?__________
    insurance?__________
14. Are house payments delinquent?__________
    How much?__________

B. *Other Real Estate*

1. Location __________
2. Type __________
3. Do you have a copy of the deed to this property? __________
4. When was it purchased? __________ Cost __________
5. Amount of downpayment __________
6. Source of downpayment __________
7. In whose name(s) is the title? __________
8. What is the present value? __________
9. Present mortgage or contract for deed balance __________
10. Monthly payment __________
11. To whom are the payments made? __________
12. Does the payment include taxes?__________
    insurance?__________
13. What are the yearly taxes?__________
    insurance?__________
14. Are house payments delinquent?__________
    How much? __________

C. *Banking*

1. Savings Account:
   Bank __________ Balance__________
   Name(s) on Account __________
2. Checking Account:
   Bank __________ Balance__________
   Name(s) on Account __________
3. Do you or your spouse have a safe deposit box __________
   Name of Bank __________

D. *Stock*

Client:
1. Company ________________ No. of Shares ________________
2. In whose name ____________ Value ________________

Spouse:
1. Company ________________ No. of Shares ________________
2. In whose name ____________ Value ________________

Joint:
1. Company ________________ No. of Shares ________________
2. In whose name ____________ Value ________________

E. *Bonds*

Client:
1. Company ________________ No. of Shares ________________
2. In whose name ____________ Value ________________

Spouse:
1. Company ________________ No. of Shares ________________
2. In whose name ____________ Value ________________

Joint:
1. Company ________________ No. of Shares ________________
2. In whose name ____________ Value ________________

F. Does anyone owe you or your spouse money? ____________
1. Who ____________________ How much ____________
2. Who ____________________ How much ____________

G. Did you or your spouse bring property or money in excess of $1,000 into this marriage? ______ Details ____________

____

H. Are any part of the assets of you or your spouse inherited? (what, when and by whom)? ____________________

____

I. Do you or your spouse have any personal injury claim pending or have you or your spouse received any settlement or award before or during your marriage (what, when and by whom)? ____________________

____

J. *Furniture and Appliances*

1. Estimated value ______________________________
2. Balance owed __________ Payments __________ Per ____
3. Payments made to whom ______________________________

K. *Motor Vehicles*

Client:

1. Make __________ Year __________ Model __________
2. In whose name? ______________________________
3. Balance owed __________ Payments __________ Per ____
4. Payments made to whom? ______________________________
5. Used by whom? ______________________________

Spouse:

1. Make __________ Year __________ Model __________
2. In whose name? ______________________________
3. Balance owed __________ Payments __________ Per ____
4. Payments made to whom? ______________________________
5. Used by whom? ______________________________

L. *Recreational Vehicles*

1. Make and model of:
   Snowmobile __________ Trailer __________
   Motorcycle __________ Boat and Motor __________
2. Estimated value of:
   Snowmobile __________ Trailer __________
   Motorcycle __________ Boat and Motor __________
3. Balance owed and monthly payments:
   Snowmobile __________ Trailer __________
   Motorcycle __________ Boat and Motor __________

M. *Other Assets*

Are there other assets that you know of? __________

____

N. *Life Insurance*

1. Company ______________________________
2. Type of Policy ______________________________
3. Name of Insured ______________________________

4. Name of Beneficiary ____________________
5. Annual Premium ____ Face Value ____ Cash Value ____

Debts (List)

Creditor	Due	Payment	Date Incurred	Party Incurring Debt

Estate

1. Do you have a Will? ______ . If so, describe any bequest for your spouse or for your children ____________________
2. When was your Will executed or last revised? __________

Miscellaneous

1. Do you or your spouse desire to have a name change as a result of this proceeding? ______ If so, what name is desired? ____________________
2. Are you or your spouse named as a party in any pending lawsuit, including bankruptcy? ____________________

CHAPTER 17

What does a Marital Termination Agreement look like?

We have included on the following pages a well-drafted stipulation, or Marital Termination Agreement. Your contract will live with you far into the future; therefore, it must be sufficiently detailed to cover eventualities. You will notice that each of the topics discussed earlier in this book is settled in the sample document: maintenance, child support, visitation, etc. Notice, too, that the husband's $100,000 pension is not split by means of a Qualified Domestic Relations Order (QDRO); instead, it is awarded to the husband alone. This reflects a negotiated exchange for the $100,000 of equity in the homestead which is awarded solely to the wife.

The better written your agreement, the less the likelihood of future disputes regarding the clarity of the agreement's terms. The equity of your bargain is a separate issue, always subject to possible dispute, but the terms and intent of the contract should be clear to any reader.

SAMPLE STIPULATION/MARITAL TERMINATION AGREEMENT

STATE OF MINNESOTA — DISTRICT COURT
COUNTY OF HENNEPIN — FOURTH JUDICIAL DISTRICT
FAMILY COURT DIVISION

In Re the Marriage of:

Court File No. 86-F-3112

David Smith,

Petitioner,

MARITAL TERMINATION AGREEMENT

and

Mary Smith,

Respondent.

WHEREAS, the above-entitled proceeding is one for dissolution of marriage commenced by the above-named Petitioner; and

WHEREAS, the Petitioner and Respondent in the above-entitled proceeding are husband and wife, respectively, and differences have arisen between them on account of which they have separated and are now living apart; and

WHEREAS, it appears to both of the parties hereto that efforts toward reconciliation would not be fruitful; and

WHEREAS, the parties are desirous of amicably settling their differences with regard to child custody, child support, maintenance, property settlement, attorneys' fees and other matters relating thereto; and

WHEREAS, the Petitioner herein is being represented in these proceedings by James Brown, Esquire, and the Respondent herein is being represented in these proceedings by Jeanette A. Frederickson, Esquire; and

WHEREAS, the Petitioner is employed by IBM, and has a gross income of $8,750 per month and a net income of $5,920 per month. The Respondent is unemployed; and

WHEREAS, the parties have a marital estate consisting of a homestead, one parcel of real property, vehicles, a retirement plan, a savings account and a checking account, and miscellaneous personal property and household goods.

NOW THEREFORE, IT IS HEREBY STIPULATED AND AGREED by and between the parties to the above-entitled proceeding as follows, to wit:

1. *Military Status.* That neither party is or has been in the military service of the United States at any time relevant to these proceedings.

2. *Complete Agreement.* That the parties have entered into this Agreement intending that it be a full, complete and final settlement and satisfaction of any and all claims of any kind, nature and description to which either party may be entitled or may claim to be entitled, now or in the future, against the other, and except as is expressly provided herein to the contrary, each is released from any and all further liability of any kind, nature or description whatsoever to the other.

3. *Default Hearing.* That the Respondent will not appear in these proceedings, save and except through the Marital Termination Agreement.

4. *Court Approval.* That the Petitioner shall proceed with said dissolution as if by default and that as a part of the proceedings in this matter, the Petitioner will submit this Agreement to the above-entitled Court. If the dissolution is not granted, the terms of this Agreement shall be of no effect, and if this Agreement is not approved by the Court, the Respondent shall be advised and shall be given the opportunity to appear and present arguments, witnesses and testimony. That if this Agreement is approved by the Court, and if the Court grants a dissolution to the Petitioner herein, the terms of this Agreement shall be made a part of any Decree issued by reference, whether or not each and every portion of this Agreement is literally set forth in the Judgment and Decree.

5. *Maintenance.* That commencing March 1, 1989, the Petitioner shall pay to the Respondent as and for maintenance the sum of Two Thousand Dollars ($2,000) per month payable in equal installments of One Thousand Dollars ($1,000) on the first

(1st) and fifteenth (15th) days of each month. Such maintenance is permanent until the Respondent's remarriage or her death, whichever occurs first.

It is intended that the amounts payable to Respondent in accordance herewith shall be includable in the Respondent's gross income pursuant to Section 71 of the Internal Revenue Code, and shall be deductible by the Petitioner pursuant to Section 215 of the Internal Revenue Code.

6. *Cost-of-Living Adjustment (COLA).* That this document is subject to the provisions of *Minnesota Statutes Section 518.641* contained in Appendix A, attached hereto and incorporated herein by reference. These provisions apply to the Two Thousand Dollars ($2,000). The COLA will be applied to the maintenance amount within the statutory time. The cost-of-living index to be applied is the Consumer Price Index for all Urban Consumers, Minneapolis-St. Paul (CPI-U).

7. *Health Insurance.* That the Petitioner shall continue the group health insurance coverage he has through his employment for the benefit of Respondent if she so desires. That said insurance carrier is required under *Minnesota Statutes Section 62A.21* and the *Consolidated Omnibus Budget Reconciliation Act of 1985 (COBRA),* P.L. 99-272, Title X, Sections 10001-10002, to continue said coverage pursuant to law and to permit the Respondent to have conversion within the statutory period. Each party shall keep the other party advised of a current mailing address so long as any such insurance is maintained. The costs of the medical and hospitalization insurance coverage obtained by the Respondent for her benefit (to the extent that it exceeds the cost for dependent coverage maintained for the benefit of the parties' minor child), shall be at the Respondent's expense, and the Petitioner shall have no obligation whatsoever to pay for the insurance coverage for the Respondent. The Petitioner shall have the costs of the same withheld from his pay, if required, subject to monthly reimbursement by the Respondent within ten (10) days of the due date of the premium. If the Respondent fails or refuses to provide payment for such insurance coverage, the Petitioner may refuse to have such sums withheld from his pay (and the insurance coverage may be terminated).

8. *Jurisdiction.* That Minnesota is the proper jurisdiction within the contemplation of the Uniform Child Custody Jurisdiction Act to enter an Order regarding the custody, care and control of the minor child.

9. *Custody.* That the parties shall have joint legal custody of their minor child, namely:

> Carol Ann Smith, born April 12, 1977, and presently twelve (12) years of age.

The Respondent shall have sole physical custody of the child subject to reasonable and liberal visitation by the Petitioner.

10. *Residency.* That neither party shall remove the minor child of the parties from the State of Minnesota for the purpose of changing her place of residence without the written consent of the other party or until further Order of the Court, so long as either party is a resident of the State of Minnesota. That if the Respondent desires to relocate to another state, the question of custody shall be reviewed, and custody shall be redetermined if appropriate.

11. *Resolution of Conflict.* That any claim or controversy arising under this Agreement involving custody or visitation which cannot be resolved by the parties through direct communication without mediation, shall be promptly submitted to mediation.

a. *Definition of Mediation.* Mediation is a voluntary process entered into by the parties. In this process, the parties continue direct communication, but with the assistance of a neutral person who is the mediator, which mediator has no authority to require any concession or agreements. A good-faith effort shall be made to resolve any claim or controversy arising between the parties.

b. *Selection of Mediator.* The mediator shall be named by mutual agreement of the parties or by obtaining a list of five qualified persons and by alternately striking names.

c. *Duties and Responsibilities of Mediator.* The mediator shall have the duty and responsibility to assist the parties in resolving all issues submitted for mediation.
d. *Duty to Cooperate and Complete.* Both parties agree to cooperate and operate in good faith to resolve the matters in dispute with the assistance of the mediator.
e. *Payment of Costs.* Both parties shall share the mediator's fees and disbursements equally unless they mutually agree otherwise. The mediator shall provide the parties with his/her fee and disbursement schedule in advance of mediation.
f. *Confidentiality and Privilege.* Within the limits of the law, the mediator will accord confidentiality and privilege to all communications with the parties.
g. *Mediator as Witness.* The mediator shall not participate as a witness, collateral contact or attorney in a custody or visitation study or inquiry involving either party. Further, neither party may ever call the mediator as a witness to testify in any proceeding involving their children or the subject matter of the mediation.
h. *Compromise or Offers to Compromise During Mediation or Arbitration.* State statute shall be applicable throughout the entire process of mediation.
i. *Applicability of Dispute Settlement Procedures.* The above procedures shall apply to any claims or controversies regarding custody or visitation.
j. *Exhaustion of Remedies.* The above procedure shall be followed before either party may apply to the Court for relief.

12. *Concealment of the Minor Child.* That this Agreement is subject to the provisions of *Minnesota Statutes Section 609.26* contained in Appendix A, attached hereto and incorporated herein by reference.

13. *Child Support.* That commencing March 1, 1989, the Petitioner shall pay to the Respondent as and for the support of the minor child, the sum of One Thousand Dollars ($1,000) per month, payable in equal installments of Five Hundred Dollars

($500) on the first (1st) and fifteenth (15th) days of each month until said minor child attains the age of eighteen (18) or age twenty (20) if said child is still attending high school, or until said minor child is emancipated, self-supporting, married, in the armed services of the United States, deceased, or until further Order of the Court, whichever occurs first.

14. *Income Tax Exemptions.* That the Petitioner shall have the right to the income tax exemption for the minor child of the parties. The Respondent shall not take any action that would affect the Petitioner's right to claim said exemption, and she shall execute any necessary documents, including waivers, to permit said exemption to be claimed in accordance herewith.

15. *Notice of Support Priority.* That this Agreement is subject to the provisions of Rule 7.01 of the Minnesota Rules of Family Court Procedure contained in Appendix A, attached hereto and incorporated herein by reference.

16. *Income Withholding.* That this Agreement is subject to the provisions of *Minnesota Statutes Section 518.611* contained in Appendix A, attached hereto and incorporated herein by reference.

17. *Docketing of Judgment for Unpaid Familial Support.* That this Agreement is subject to the provisions of *Minnesota Statutes Section 518.091* contained in Appendix A, attached hereto and incorporated herein by reference.

18. *Notice of Address or Residence Change.* That this Agreement is subject to the provisions of *Minnesota Statutes Section 518.55, subd. 3,* contained in Appendix A, attached hereto and incorporated herein by reference.

19. *Health Insurance for the Minor Child.* That during the time that a child of the parties is a minor, the Petitioner shall provide major medical and hospitalization insurance available through his employment (at no cost or at nominal cost) for the benefit of the minor child. The Petitioner shall be responsible for all deductible and non-insured medical and dental expenses of the minor child. This Agreement is subject to the provisions of *Minnesota Statutes Section 518.171* contained in Appendix A, attached hereto and incorporated herein by reference.

20. *Life Insurance.* That the Petitioner shall keep and maintain in full force and effect a policy or policies of life insurance on himself, naming the Respondent beneficiary thereof, in an amount not less than his projected future child support and maintenance obligations herein until the Petitioner is no longer obligated to provide familial support.

21. *Homestead.* That the Respondent is hereby awarded all right, title, interest and equity in and to the homestead of the parties located at 1007 South 73rd Street, in the City of Minneapolis, County of Hennepin, State of Minnesota, and legally described as follows:

Lots 6 and 7, Auditor's Subdivision No. 77.

Such interest shall be free and clear of any claim on the part of the Petitioner.

That Respondent shall be solely liable for all monthly payments of principal, interest, taxes and insurance on said homestead, and she shall indemnify and hold Petitioner harmless from any liability or obligation to make any payment whatsoever regarding said homestead. The homestead has a fair market value of $200,000 and is presently encumbered by a mortgage of $100,000 in favor of First Bank Federal.

22. *Six-Plex.* That the Petitioner is hereby awarded all right, title, interest and equity in and to the six-plex of the parties located at 4721 France Avenue South, in the City of Minneapolis, County of Hennepin, State of Minnesota, and legally described as follows:

> Lot 16, Block 4, according to the Plat thereof on file and of record in the office of the County Recorder of Hennepin County, located on Plat 7743, Parcel 216, subject to covenants, easements and restrictions of record.

Such interest shall be free and clear of any claim on the part of the Respondent.

That the Petitioner shall be solely liable for all monthly payments of principal, interest, taxes and insurance on said property, and he shall indemnify and hold the Respondent harmless from any liability or obligation to make any payment whatsoever regarding said property. The six-plex has a fair market value of $250,000 and is presently encumbered by a mortgage of $225,000 in favor of First Bank Federal.

23. *Household Goods and Furnishings.* That the Petitioner is hereby awarded all right, title, interest and equity, free and clear of any claim on the part of the Respondent, in and to the household goods, furnishings, jewelry, and all other tangible personal property in the Petitioner's possession. In addition, the Petitioner is awarded:

a. 1988 Volvo automobile;
b. sailboat;
c. 1988 Honda Goldwing motorcycle; and
d. oil painting collection.

That the Respondent is awarded all right, title, interest and equity, free and clear of any claim on the part of the Petitioner, in and to the household goods, furnishings, jewelry, and all other tangible personal property in the Respondent's possession.

24. *Bank Accounts and Investments.* That the Petitioner is hereby awarded all right, title, interest and equity, free and clear of any claim on the part of the Respondent, in and to any cash, savings or checking accounts, stocks, bonds and dividends in the Petitioner's name or under his control.

That the Respondent is hereby awarded all right, title, interest and equity, free and clear of any claim on the part of the Respondent, in and to any cash, savings or checking accounts, stocks, bonds and dividends in Respondent's name or under her control.

That the Petitioner agrees to pay to Respondent one-half of the existing cash value of the New England Life Insurance Policy valued at $20,224 as of March 1, 1989. Petitioner will pay to Respondent $10,112 upon obtaining a loan on the policy for that amount.

25. *Retirement Interests.* That the Petitioner is hereby awarded all right, title, interest and equity, free and clear of any claim on the part of the Respondent, in and to any and all profit sharing, pension and retirement interests in his name, specifi-

cally including the Petitioner's IBM Pension Plan, valued at $100,000.

26. *Automobiles.* That the Petitioner is hereby awarded all right, title, interest and equity, free and clear of any claim on the part of the Respondent, in and to the 1987 BMW automobile of the parties. The Petitioner shall assume any encumbrances thereon, and he shall indemnify and hold the Respondent harmless from any obligation to pay the same. The Respondent shall, upon entry of the Judgment and Decree, or sooner if she desires, execute all necessary documents to effect transfer of the title.

That the Respondent is hereby awarded all right, title, interest and equity, free and clear of any claim on the part of the Petitioner, in and to the 1988 Toyota automobile. The Respondent shall assume any encumbrances thereon, and she shall indemnify and hold the Petitioner harmless from any obligation to pay the same.

27. *Income Tax Returns.* That the Petitioner and the Respondent shall file joint state and federal income tax returns for the calendar year 1988. The Petitioner shall assume any liability for the filing of said returns. However, the parties shall share equally in any refunds from the filing of their 1988 joint state and federal income tax returns.

28. *Joint Debts.* That the parties have satisfied all bills and obligations of the parties incurred during the marriage, not otherwise specified herein, which constitute a joint obligation of the parties except the following:

VISA $5,000.

That the Petitioner shall assume and pay the above-stated debt to VISA, and he shall indemnify and hold the Respondent harmless from any obligation to make payment of the same.

29. *Separate Debts.* That the Petitioner shall assume and pay the debts which he has incurred since January 1, 1987, which are not otherwise specified herein, and he shall indemnify and hold the Respondent harmless from any obligation to make payment of the same.

That the Respondent shall assume and pay the debts which she has incurred since January 1, 1987, which are not otherwise specified herein, and she shall indemnify and hold the Petitioner harmless from any obligation to make payment of the same.

30. *Undisclosed Debts*. That in the event that there is a debt obligation that has not been heretofore disclosed, that obligation shall become the sole responsibility of the party who incurred it.

31. *Attorneys' Fees*. That the Petitioner shall be responsible for his attorneys' fees and costs incurred incident to this proceeding.

That the Respondent shall be responsible for her attorney's fees and costs incurred incident to this proceeding.

32. *Service of the Judgment and Decree*. That service of a copy of the final Judgment and Decree herein may be made upon the Petitioner's attorney, James Brown, Esquire, Suite 123, 10 Third Avenue South, Minneapolis, Minnesota 55401, by United States mail, and the same shall be in lieu of personal service upon the Petitioner.

That service of a copy of the final Judgment and Decree herein may be made upon Respondent's attorney, Jeanette A. Frederickson, Esquire, Chestnut & Brooks, P.A., 3700 Piper Jaffray Tower, 222 South Ninth Street, Minneapolis, Minnesota 55402, by United States mail, and the same shall be in lieu of personal service upon the Respondent.

33. *Future Interpretation*. That paragraph headings are for convenience only. They are not part of the Agreement of the parties and shall not be used in the construction thereof.

That this Marital Termination Agreement is not to be strictly construed for or against either of the parties. It shall be interpreted simply and fairly to both parties.

34. *Execution and Exchange of Documents*. That to implement the terms and provisions contained herein, each of the parties shall make, execute and deliver to the other party instruments of conveyance, assignment and other documents as may be required. In the event either party fails to do so, the Judgment and Decree shall operate as said conveyance.

35. *Full Disclosure and Reliance.* That each party warrants to the other that there has been accurate, complete and current disclosure of all income, assets, debts and liabilities.

36. *Acknowledgement of Agreement.* That the parties have read this Agreement, have given it serious thought and consideration, and understand its contents. That this Agreement is fair, just and equitable under the circumstances, and it has been made in aid of an orderly and just determination of the property settlement in this matter satisfactory to both parties. This Agreement is being entered into by the parties subsequent to the definite understanding between them that there can be no reconciliation.

37. *Release.* That subject to the foregoing and subject to full compliance therewith, each of the parties does in all respects, manners and things release and fully discharge the other from any liability, claims or obligations of any kind or character, whether arising out of the marriage relationship or otherwise, and the foregoing shall be deemed to constitute a full, final and complete property settlement between the parties.

IT IS FURTHER STIPULATED AND AGREED, that this Agreement may be approved by the Court without notice to the parties.

DATE__________________	DATE__________________
______________________	______________________
David Smith, Petitioner	Mary Smith, Respondent
DATE__________________	DATE__________________
______________________	______________________
James Brown Suite 123 10 Third Avenue South Minneapolis, MN 55401 (612) 123-4567	Jeanette A. Frederickson Chestnut & Brooks, P.A. 3700 Piper Jaffray Tower 222 South Ninth Street Minneapolis, MN 55402 (612) 339-7300
Attorney for Petitioner	Attorney for Respondent

CHAPTER 18

What should I do if there is violence in our home?

Each year in Minnesota approximately 43,000 women are assaulted by their husbands or partners. It is a nationwide problem of enormous proportions, and the reasons this phenomena exists and perpetuates itself have been examined carefully only in the past 15 years. Domestic abuse occurs in families of all social, economic and educational backgrounds.

Once violence begins, it tends to increase in severity and frequency. The abused woman cannot control the batterer, though she thinks she can, and only intervention can stop the escalating violence. Violence is a learned behavior which is defined by the legislature in this way:

i. physical harm, bodily injury, assault or the infliction of fear of imminent physical harm, bodily injury or assault, between family or household members; or
ii. criminal sexual conduct, within the meanings of sections 609.342, 609.343, 609.344, or 609.345, committed against a minor family or household member by an adult family or household member.

Minnesota Statutes Section 518B.01, subd. 2(a) (1988).

Violence and threats can be used by men to reduce their stress levels, gain power and punish others. Inflicting violence can provide momentary stress release which results in control of a partner or situation. A woman who lives in fear of violence will alter her behavior to avoid it.

Studies show that battered women are frequently from "traditional" families, in which the women are economically and psychologically dependent on men and tend to accommodate the husband's demands. She may mistakenly feel that her husband has the right to discipline her if she falls short in her duties or does not perform to his satisfaction.

If such a woman is emotionally or psychologically dependent on her husband, then she may feel that keeping her family together is her highest priority. As a result, she will absorb much punishment to avoid societal discovery. Ashamed, she will be reluctant to admit, even to herself, that her husband is a batterer, let alone report him for the deed.

As a result, the husband learns that the family is a safe place to be violent. His frustration and anger are reduced through his harmful physical acts, yet society seldom interferes with this private violence.

Batterers were frequently abused themselves as children and often suffer from low self-esteem. A batterer is dependent upon his wife, whom he controls and beats. She, in turn, lives in a state of learned helplessness, dependent on him, financially and psychologically entrapped.

If there is violence in your household and you want to take action, help is available. You must first protect yourself physically. If you feel you have no friends or relatives who can help you, or that a move to another household will not stop the abuser, there are a number of shelters or "safe houses" available in Minnesota. You can locate the one closest to you by calling a Help Line, such as "First Call for Help," or your local police or social welfare agency. A comprehensive list of Minnesota programs is given at the end of this Chapter.

In 1978 Minnesota passed the Domestic Abuse Act, which gave a spouse the means of obtaining quick and effective help in the form of a "Petition for an Order for Protection." This Act covers domestic violence between either related or unrelated persons living in the same household. It applies to spouses; former spouses; parents and children; persons related by blood and persons who are living together or who have lived together; and any persons who have parented a child, regardless of marital status. The petition may be made by any household member on his own behalf or on behalf of any minor in the household.

Most counties have forms available to applicants who are filing for an order for protection. You must be able clearly and specifically to describe the violence. A social worker will assess whether your complaint merits the protection granted by the statute and present your statement to a judge for review. If the judge agrees that there is recent and serious violence, he or she will sign an order requiring the person accused to leave the home immediately and not return until after a hearing. The police, or the sheriff, will serve this order on the party to be removed, and see to it that the person leaves the residence immediately.

Within five days, both parties must appear in court at the date and time set forth in the first order. If you apply for an order and fail to appear in court, the matter will be dismissed, but it may be more difficult to get this protection the second time.

If you are the one served with an order and fail to appear, an order can be issued which bars you from the household, or a warrant can be issued for your arrest; the judge will make this decision. This order can remain in effect either until you appear or for one full year. Whether you are a applying for an order or are served with one, you may wish to consult an attorney to help you through this process. If the support, custody or visitation of a child is affected by excluding one party from the home, the court may consider those issues at the hearing.

At the first hearing, the parties may agree that an order for protection should be entered. This can be done without the accused admitting responsibility for any violence. Such an order will then provide immediate police protection if any problems subsequently arise. People who have already separated often agree to the entry of such an order because it does not require a party to leave the home.

An order for protection can be contested at an evidentiary hearing. There is an absolute right to such a hearing if one party requests it. When an evidentiary hearing is granted, it is usually scheduled a few days after the first hearing, and the initial order remains in effect.

The Domestic Abuse Act offers extensive protection for a victim of battering. It may:

a. restrain any party from committing acts of domestic abuse;

b. exclude the abusing party from the dwelling which the parties share or from the residence of the petitioner;
c. award temporary custody or establish temporary visitation with regard to minor children of the parties on a basis which gives primary consideration to the safety of the victim and the children. If the court finds that the safety of the victim or the children will be jeopardized by unsupervised or unrestricted visitation, the court shall condition or restrict visitation as to time, place, duration, or supervision, or deny visitation entirely, as needed to guard the safety of the victim and the children. The court's deliberation under this subdivision shall in no way delay the issuance of an order for protection granting other reliefs provided for in Laws 1985, chapter 1985;
d. on the same basis as is provided in chapter 518, establish temporary support for minor children or a spouse, and order the withholding of support from the income of the person obligated to pay the support according to chapter 518;
e. provide upon request of the petitioner counselling or other social services for the parties, if married, or if there are minor children;
f. order the abusing party to participate in treatment or counselling services;
g. award temporary use and possession of property and restrain one or both parties from transferring, encumbering, concealing, or disposing of property except in the usual course of business or for the necessities of life, and to account to the court for all such transfers, encumbrances, dispositions, and expenditures, made after the order is served or communicated to the parties restrained in open court; or
h. order, in its discretion, other relief as the court deems necessary for the protection of a family or household member, including orders or directives to the sheriff or constable.

Minnesota Statutes Section 518B.01, subd. 6(a-h) (1988).

With an order for protection in place, a court may order various forms of relief. It may:

a. restrain any party from committing acts of domestic abuse;
b. exclude the abusing party from the dwelling which the parties share;
c. award temporary custody or establish temporary visitation with regard to minor children;
d. establish temporary support for minor children or for a spouse;
e. provide counselling or other social services for the parties if married or if there are minor children;
f. order the abusing party to participate in treatment or counselling services; or
g. order, in its discretion, other relief as the Court deems necessary for the protection of a family or household member, including orders or directive to the sheriff or constable.

Remember that community intervention is available to guide victims through the court process. Advocates will coordinate the efforts of police and social service agencies in developing effective intervention strategies. However, you must place that first call. See the extensive list which follows to locate the help nearest you.

WOMEN'S SHELTERS

Northwestern Minnesota

Ripley Shelter
(Thief River Falls)
218/681-5596
681-5557

Project Safe
(Crookston)
218/281-2864

Northwoods Coalition Shelter
(Bemidji)
218/751-6346
751-0211

Stevens County Battered Women's Committee
(Morris)
612/589-1481

Women's Crisis Center Shelter
(Fergus Falls)
218/739-3486
739-3359

SAFE
(Wadena)
218/631-1714
631-4357

Women's Center of Mid-Minnesota Shelter
(Brainerd)
218/828-1216
(Business/Crisis)

Northeastern Minnesota

Aitkin County Women's Advocates
(Aitkin)
218/768-3701
828-1216

Cook County Women's Advocates
(Grand Marais)
218/387-1137
(Business/Crisis)

Rural Women's Advocates
(Cloquet)
218/389-6065
800/232-1300

Domestic Abuse Intervention Project
(Duluth)
218/722-2781
722-4134

Friends Against Abuse
(International Falls)
218/285-7220
283-9844

Battered Women's Program/Itasca Co.
(Grand Rapids)
218/326-0388
326-8565

North Shore Horizons
(Two Harbors)
218/834-5924
800/232-1300

Range Women's Advocates
(Chisholm)
218/254-3377
800/232-1300

Women's Coalition
Shelter
(Duluth)
218/728-6481
800/232-1300

Central Minnesota

Mille Lacs County Family
Services
(Milaca)
612/938-6161

Minnesota Migrant
Council
(St. Cloud)
612/253-7010
(Business/Crisis)
*Spanish Spoken

Woman House Shelter
(St. Cloud)
612/253-6900
252-1603

Refuge
(Cambridge)
612/689-3532

WINDOW
(Sandstone)
612/245-5224

Alexandra House Shelter
(Blaine)
612/780-2332
780-2330

BIHA, Women in Action
(Minneapolis)
612/870-1193

Casa de Esperanza
Shelter
(St. Paul)
612/772-1723
772-1611
*Spanish spoken

Cornerstone Advocacy
Service
(Bloomington)
612/884-0330
884-0376

Center for Domestic
Abuse
(St. Paul)
612/641-5584
(Business/Crisis)

Domestic Abuse Project
(Minneapolis)
612/874-7063
(Business/Crisis)

Eastside Neighborhood
Services
(Minneapolis)
612/781-6011

Education for
Cooperative Living
(Minneapolis)
612/521-3646
(Business/Crisis)

Family Violence Network
(Lake Elmo)
612/770-8544
770-0777

Family Violence Program
Division of Indian Work
(Minneapolis)
612/827-1795
(Business/Crisis)

Harriet Tubman Women's
Shelter
(Minneapolis)
612/827-6105
827-2841

Home Free Shelter
(Plymouth)
612/559-9008
559-4945

Indian Health Board
(Minneapolis)
612/721-3200
(Business/Crisis)

Lewis House Shelter
(Eagan)
612/452-7466
452-7288

IBCA Battered Women's
Program
(Minneapolis)
612/871-7878
(Business/Crisis)

IBCA Battered Women's
Program
(St. Paul)
612/227-0299
(Business/Crisis)

Family & Children's
Services
(Minneapolis)
612/340-7444

Crime Victim Center
(Minneapolis)
612/340-5432
340-5400

Community University
Health Care Center
(Minneapolis)
612/627-4774
*Service to Southeast
Asians

Sojourner Shelter
(Hopkins)
612/933-7433
933-7422

Southern Valley Alliance
for Battered Women
(Belle Plaine)
612/873-4212
(Business/Crisis)

St. Paul Intervention
Project
(St. Paul)
612/645-2824

Wilder Community
Assistance Program
(St. Paul)
612/221-0048
(Business/Crisis)

Women of Nations
(St. Paul)
612/292-9358
292-9487

Women's Advocates
Shelter
(St. Paul)
612/227-9966
227-8284

WomanKind
(Minneapolis)
612/924-5775

YMCA "Women
Emerging"
Transitional Housing
(St. Paul)
612/293-9296

United Battered Families
Network
(Bloomington)
612/881-1872

Southwestern Minnesota

Shelter House
(Willmar)
612/235-4613
800/992-1716

New WAV (Women
Against Violence)
(Worthington)
507/376-4311

Southwest Women's
Shelter
(Marshall)
507/532-4604
532-2350

Southeastern Minnesota

CADA House Shelter
(Mankato)
507/625-8688
625-7233

Domestic Abuse
Advocates of Wabasha
County
(Plainview)
507/534-2234

Freeborn County Victims'
Crisis Center
(Albert Lee)
507/373-2223

Houston County Women's
Resources
(Caledonia)
507/724-2676

Mower County Crime
Victim Crisis Center
(Austin)
507-433-7389
437-6680

Women's Resources
Center
(Winona)
507/452-4440
(Business/Crisis)

Women's Shelter
(Rochester)
507/285-1010

YMCA Women's
Resources Center
(Rochester)
507/289-0638

Bibliography

The Complete Legal Guide to Marriage, Divorce, Custody and Living Together. Steven Mitchell Sack. New York: McGraw-Hill Book Company, 1987.

Consultation with a Divorce Lawyer. Bernard E. Clau and Anthony R. Daniele. New York: Simon & Schuster, 1982.

Divorce: The Man's Complete Guide to Winning. Lauren O. Vail. New York: Sovereign Books, 1979.

The Divorce Decision: The Legal Consequences of Ending a Marriage. Richard Neely. New York: McGraw-Hill Book Company, 1984.

The Divorce Handbook: Your Basic Guide to Divorce. James T. Friedman. New York: Random House, 1982.

The Divorce Revolution: The Unexpected Social & Economic Consequences for Women and Children in America. Lenore Weitzman. New York: Free Press Publishing Co./Collier MacMillan, 1985.

The Dollars and Sense of Divorce. Judith Briles. New York: Master Media Limited, 1988.

Everything You Want to Know About Your Husband's Money... & Need to Know Before the Divorce. Shelley Aspaklaria and Gerson Geltner. New York: T.Y. Crowell, 1980.

Minnesota Family Law Primer. Robert E. Oliphant. St. Paul, MN: Creative Legal Communications, Inc., 1988.

Second Chances: Men, Women and Children a Decade After Divorce. Dr. Judith Wallerstein and Sandra Blakeslee. New York: Ticknor & Fields, 1989.

What Every Man Should Know About Divorce. Robert Cassidy. Washington, D.C.: New Republic Books, 1977.

A Woman's Guide to Divorce and Decision Making. Christina Robertson. New York: Simon & Schuster, 1988.

A Woman's Legal Guide to Separation and Divorce in all 50 States. Norma Aurwood. New York: Scribner, 1985.

Glossary

These words are defined by their most common usage in divorce actions.

ACTION (Same as Cause of Action). Another term for a lawsuit.

AFFIDAVIT. A written statement of facts made under oath and signed before a notary public.

AGREEMENT. The oral or written resolution of disputed issues that is incorporated into a court order, judgment or decree.

ALIMONY. Spousal support; same as maintenance.

ALLEGATION. A statement of facts in a pleading; what the pleader intends to prove.

APPEAL. The process whereby a superior court reviews the proceedings in a lower court to determine whether there was reversible error. The appellate court can amend the judgment or remand the case to the lower court for a new trial.

APPEARANCE. The physical presence of a party at a court hearing; formal submission to a court's jurisdiction.

CLAIM. A charge by one spouse against the other.

COMPLAINT. The initial pleading in a divorce action stating the allegations upon which the requested relief is based. In Minnesota this is called a petition.

CONTEMPT OF COURT. The willful failure to comply with a court order, judgment or decree.

CONTESTED CASE. Any case where the court must decide one or more issues that are not agreed to by the parties. All cases are considered contested until all issues are resolved by agreement of the parties.

CROSS-EXAMINATION. The questioning of a witness by the opposing party at a deposition or trial, to test the truth of his/her testimony or to develop it further.

DECREE. The final ruling of the judge in an action for divorce, legal separation, or annulment; same as judgment.

DEFAULT ORDER or DEFAULT JUDGMENT. An order or judgment given by the court when the opposition failed to plead within the time allowed or failed to appear at the hearing (this may be by agreement).

DEFENDANT. The one who defends the lawsuit brought by another; same as respondent.

DEPOSITION. The sworn testimony of a witness taken out of court and reduced to writing. Discovery depositions are often taken for the purpose of discovering the facts or discovering the substance of a witness' testimony prior to trial. The deposition may be used to discredit a witness if he changes his testimony. Evidence depositions are used to preserve the testimony of a witness who will be unable to appear at trial.

DIRECT EXAMINATION. The initial questioning of a witness by the attorney who called him to testify.

DISCOVERY. Procedures used by attorneys to determine the nature, scope and credibility of the opposing party's claim. Such procedures include depositions and written interrogatories. Psychological examinations and court social service investigations are also part of discovery.

DISCRETION OF THE COURT. The area of choice a judge exercises to make a legally acceptable decision on his or her interpretation of the evidence.

EMANCIPATION. The point at which a minor child comes of age. In Minnesota it occurs when a child reaches 18 or 21, or upon marriage, full-time employment or entering the armed services. Emancipation terminates the duty to support.

EQUITABLE DIVISION OF PROPERTY. A system of dividing property acquired by spouses during their marriage.

EVIDENCE. Documents, testimony or other demonstrative material offered to the court to prove or disprove allegations in the pleadings.

EX PARTE. The application for court relief without the presence of the other party, due either to a lack of notice or the choice of the other party not to appear.

HEARING. Any proceeding before the court where testimony is taken or arguments offered by the attorneys for the purpose of resolving disputed issues.

IMPEACHMENT. The act of proving that a witness is inaccurate, confused, misinformed, biased or lying, either by using prior admissions, inconsistent statements or other conflicting evidence.

INDEMNIFICATION. To promise to reimburse another person in case of an anticipated loss.

INJUNCTION. A court order forbidding someone from doing a particular act which is likely to cause physical or mental injury or property loss to another person.

INTERROGATORIES. A series of written questions served upon the opposing party to discover facts regarding the disputed issues.

JOINT PROPERTY. Property held in the name of more than one person.

JUDGMENT. The order of the court on a disputed issue; same as decree.

JURISDICTION. The power of the court to rule upon issues relating to the parties, their children or their property.

LEGAL SEPARATION. A cause of action for support while the spouses are living apart. Legal separation provides for maintenance, child custody and support, but does not divide property. A decree of legal separation does not dissolve the marriage and does not allow the parties to remarry.

MAINTENANCE. Spousal support; same as alimony.

MARITAL PROPERTY. All income and property (regardless of who holds title) acquired by the spouses during the course of their marriage, with the exception of property acquired by inheritance or gift.

MOTION. A written or oral application to the court for some particular relief, such as temporary support, injunction, or attorneys' fees.

NO-FAULT DIVORCE. Under the Minnesota system, divorce is granted without the necessity of proving marital misconduct.

ORDER. The court's ruling on a disputed issue requiring the parties to do certain things or setting forth their rights and responsibilities. The order is reduced to writing and may be signed by the judge and filed with the court by agreement, without a court hearing.

PERSONAL JURISDICTION. The power of the court to order a spouse to do a particular thing such as pay spousal maintenance or child support.

PETITION. A written application for particular relief from the court. In Minnesota, a complaint for divorce is entitled "Petition for Dissolution of Marriage."

PLEADING. Formal written application to the court for relief and the written response. Pleadings include complaints, answers, petitions, responses, motions, and all counter-pleadings.

RESPONSE. The pleading filed in answer to a petition.

SETTLEMENT. The agreed resolution of disputed issues.

SETTLEMENT AGREEMENT. The settlement reduced to a written document or agreed to in open court.

SHOW CAUSE. A contempt-of-court proceeding to enforce court orders, judgment or decrees which have been violated. The alleged violator is given an opportunity to show why he should not be held in contempt.

STIPULATION. An agreement between the parties or their counsel resolving some or all of the disputed issues.

SUBPOENA. A document served upon a person who is not a party to the action, requiring him to appear and give testimony at a deposition or court hearing.

SUMMONS. A written notification to the defendant that an action has been commenced requiring him to respond within a specified period of time.

TEMPORARY MOTIONS. Application to the court for interim relief pending the final decree of divorce, separate maintenance, or annulment. Typical temporary motions include: temporary maintenance, child support, attorneys' fees, custody, visitation, or enforcement or modification of prior temporary orders. The court enters a temporary order after a hearing.

TESTIMONY. Statements made under oath by a witness in a court hearing or deposition.

TRIAL. A formal court hearing to decide disputed issues raised by the pleadings.

VACATED. If a court order, judgment or decree is found defective, it is eliminated, and either a substitute order is entered or a new hearing is granted.